Mam, 1972

In my memory the room is white. Bright white. There is a door and in the door is a square. In the square there is a pane of glass and in the glass there is a face.

I am in a cot and the cot is cold. I am standing – holding on. A baby is asleep in the cot beside me. I can't see him – I think it is a him – I can just see his bulk covered by blankets. He is a baby, but I am not.

The face comes into the room and the pane of glass turns green in the white door. The face is coming towards me and its body is holding something. The body of the face is giving me a packet of smarties. I take them and I ask why the face is giving them to me. The face becomes a woman and she tells me that my mother has sent them. She tells me that my mother wouldn't come in. I start to open my smarties and the woman walks away. She goes to the other cot and moves the blankets and the baby moves also. I am trying to eat my smarties but I am crying instead. I have a pain between my legs and I am afraid. The woman leaves the cot with the baby and comes to me. She is telling me that I will be fine, that I am not to cry, that I might wake her baby. I feel wrong for crying and I feel wrong for trying to wake the baby. I don't belong here and I am scared. The pain between my legs is worse and I squeeze my legs to make it go away.

The woman is sitting beside her baby in the cot. She is looking at the baby and she is looking at me when I look at her. I feel alone. The pain is gone now and I pull the covers up and lie down facing a white wall. I can't see the woman and her baby and I try not to breathe – I don't want to make the woman cross. I close my eyes tight and I start to think. I close my eyes tighter because I want to stop thinking.

*   *   *

My grandmother tells me what is right and what is wrong. Chrissie is my Daddy's aunt and she tells me as well. When they tell me they whisper and when they stop telling me they talk out loud. They love me and I feel safe and happy with them. They tell me that I am a good boy and that I am full of fun. Chrissie says that I am the greatest rogue God ever made. She loves me like she loved my Daddy. She tells me that she thought that she could never have loved a child as much as that again. She tells me that I have the most beautiful brown eyes and the whitest teeth that she ever saw in a child. I feel warm when I am with her and I can do whatever I like, because their home is my home and children are supposed to do whatever they like when they are at home. In the bath Chrissie washes my hair and my back. She even washes my toes. I wash everywhere else, because that is right and anything else would be wrong.

*   *   *

The bathroom in our house is square, like the window in the white room. The toilet is in the corner, on the right. Chrissie taught me my right from my left, but I get confused. I have to think of my left first, and because the bath is to my left I can figure out that the toilet is to my right. I am in the bath with my brother. He is bigger, so I have to sit under the taps. Sometimes I hit off the hot tap and I get burned. I don't cry, because I will get slapped if I cry. My mother is washing me and she is very cross. She is pulling me and roaring at me. She asks me why I can't be good like my brother. She tells me that she will tell the Parish Priest all about me and she will tell the teacher in September that I am a bold boy who tells lies and is nothing but trouble. She says that she will tell the doctor and the lady in the chemist that I am the greatest trouble in her life. She gave her life's blood for me and I have caused her nothing but trouble. She pulls at me and she squeezes and she tells me I am a bold boy and cries 'Why can't you be like your brother!' I am shaking and I am afraid to say anything. My little man is dirty, she says, and it will get all infected if I don't wash it properly and keep it away from dirty toilets. She says that she will never teach me – I will never learn. She has so much on her plate. She has my father and she has me, who was sent to make her life difficult. She washes around my little man and I am holding my breath and I am holding in my tummy. I am supposed to feel clean, but I feel dirty instead.

*   *   *

The lady in the shop is asking my mother how she is. My mother is telling her that her heart is broken having to put up with me and, as for my father, he is wearing her down altogether. She says that only for my brother she'd be lost. She is lucky to have him. He is a good boy and never looks for anything. She says that I am a bold boy and that she caught me robbing her bag. She tells the lady that if ever I come to buy something the money will be stolen and to confiscate it. I remembered Chrissie had given me money and I was afraid in case she found it. I would be beaten, because she would say I stole it and that the whole parish would be talking about her son the thief. It was her social duty to warn everybody about me in case they tried to blame her when they found out what I was like. Everyone would know that she had done her best but that nature had dealt her a cruel blow.

She is telling the lady in the shop that I am starting school in September and that at least then she would have a break from

7

me. She tells the lady that she is killed from bringing me to doctors. My kidneys are bad, my chest is bad – I am bad. I am costing her a fortune. The lady looked at me when my mother wasn't looking and she winked at me. I felt the heat in my face and I turned away.

*   *   *

It was Saturday again and I was afraid. Saturday night was bath night.

Dad, 1973

He was shaking and his lips moved, but no sound came. My mother looked angry and I was afraid. Her lips were tight and the knuckles on her brown hands were white.

Everything seemed strange. It was a happy day, but nobody was smiling.

My sister was in the corner, between the two doors. Her chair was pink for a girl, and her dress was white for an angel. I sat on the inside, facing my brother. He was big; he was half my life older than me. I couldn't wait to be six, but he said I'd always be smaller; I'd never catch up.

'Stop acting like a child,' my mother said sternly.

I was a child, so I knew she wasn't talking to me, but I was still afraid. My father tried to answer, but he just dribbled instead.

'Hurry up and eat your breakfast,' she roared at me. I felt the wet between my legs and I wanted to cry. My brother looked at me as if I had done something wrong. I wondered if he knew.

Dad was still shaking and his hands covered his face. I wanted to hug him, but I knew I couldn't.

The church was cold and it was summer. My shorts were cold as well and the wet had made them stiff. My grandfather was there, and my uncles and aunts.

The priest came out; he was dressed in white like my sister. I held my Dad's hand. He had stopped shaking. I was tiny beside him, he was a giant. I should have felt safe, but I didn't. I wanted to be beside my grandfather, but my brother was there.

The priest poured water on my sister and everyone smiled except Dad and me. My mother looked at us and she stopped smiling. I was afraid again.

'Smile for the camera,' my uncle said. I tried to smile, but I was thinking too hard. I don't think Dad smiled either.

We went home and I went to my room. Dad went to his.

The next day Dad went to hospital. I heard them say it was for the best, but my mother was crying. I asked my brother what was happening. He told me to shut up and he hit me. I ran to the bathroom, but I was wet when I got there.

I was a big boy when my dad came home.

PART ONE

Night

Virginity

The average man remembers when he lost his virginity. He can, I am told, remember who she was, where it happened and how he felt. It would appear that I am not an average man. I have no recollection, whatsoever, of my first true sexual encounter. This inability to recall such a momentous occasion does not fill me with regret. Nor do I feel as if I have missed out on a true human experience. I was probably drunk and awkward, with someone I am glad I don't remember, and most likely quite useless.

My memories of those adolescent, formative years, when one is striving to embrace life and a multiplicity of new experiences, are quite different to the aforementioned average man. In fact, I think I skipped adolescence and went straight for adulthood. However, I did so in a manner that caused much hardship and much bitterness. That said, my options were few. I came from an environment where survival was a solitary quest. Opportunities had to be created, they were never presented. Living was a threat, and survival meant that I had to pre-empt that threat. I didn't always succeed, and hard was the experience and bitter the memory.

I was the second in a family of four children. I wish I had been the first. Maybe then it wouldn't have been as hard, and I might not be as bitter. In our house there was no such thing as security. Money was tight, religion was rife, and I was a sinner. My morals were bad: I was a republican and I smoked. Most of the time I played the game, but every so often my humanity surfaced, and with it came suffering.

I was beaten, terrorised, threatened, intimidated and, above all, I was humiliated. Nothing ever stayed behind closed doors; except the beatings, of course.

The head teacher, the parish priest, the neighbours and other religious fanatics, as well as the local doctor, were all kept informed. The intention was that I would be scorned, my family pitied and my poor suffering mother beatified. This plan didn't work, however, and we were laughed at instead.

I lived on the edge. I considered the repercussions before I took action and where possible I concealed my actions. To get carried away on a wave of enjoyment was a luxury I could not afford. Everything had to be planned.

Occasionally I trusted, but I did so at my peril, for I faced betrayal every time. Many times I would find myself locked out of the house and I would have to sleep rough. I would subsequently have to plead to be allowed home, and the terms were never negotiable.

My sibling was more my parent than my brother. He was enemy number one and I hated him.

He worked tirelessly to ingratiate himself. It would not have been so bad if he had just informed on me, but he was also adept at torture, and his speciality was mental torture. Often he would defer the physical, when he knew he had made a good discovery. On these occasions he used to wait until he could report the misdemeanour before meting out the punishment. The advantage of this was that he could glean hours of pleasure from watching me squirm as I wondered what punishment I would get from my father or mother, before he administered his.

I grew up convinced it was all one big conspiracy and that, even when they were being nice, they were just pretending.

I needed to escape. A quick shag in some dark corner wouldn't do the trick. The effort involved would be too great and the benefits too short-lived. I needed a more engrossing and lasting solution. I wanted total removal from my world and deliverance to a magical world where I could be alone, untouchable and whatever I wanted to be. My purpose was survival, my solution – drink.

*   *   *

I remember, with the greatest affection, that first drink. When my friends talk of their first sexual encounter, I close my eyes and think of mine: that first time, when I lifted the glass, its contents black and mysterious, to my lips.

The pub was an old, dilapidated imitation of traditional Ireland. It was situated on the banks of the Cloister River and had a reputation for being the watering hole of both artistic and legal minds. This combination of thinkers and dreamers was immensely attractive to me and the ambience they created only served to enhance the entire experience.

I clearly recall asking for and receiving my pint. The barmaid's name was Sinéad and, in true traditional fashion, she was heavy in a buxom type of way, freckled and formerly a redhead. Her poise was aristocratic and her demeanour was rather distant. She was, of course, in no doubt that she was in control. She held the keys to the kingdom of release and escape. She had the power: the power to serve or not to serve.

Those that were already slaves to drink were but pawns with whom she played. They pandered to her every whim, attempting to gain her favour, hoping to find solace. They were secure in the knowledge that she would never refuse them, so long as they had money in their pockets.

The others – the cute bastards, the ones that pretend to drink while really sipping and pacing themselves – unnerved

15

her. They didn't need her. They were there because they had nowhere else to go. Once they got a better offer they were gone, to a restaurant, theatre, club, or, if they were really lucky, to a willing female's flat. To these she played host, knowing that the longer they stayed the more likely they would be to become her slaves. The drink would create a desire for more, the spell would be cast and only closing time, poverty or a coma would break it.

I unsettled her. I was new, an unknown quantity. All heads turned as she analysed me, attempting to uncover my pedigree. Was I an itinerant, a bum, from the right side of town? Was I under-age? Did she want to serve me? Would she demonstrate her power and refuse me?

All eyes left me and turned to her. It was her call; she was judge, jury and executioner.

'Can I help you?' she asked.

The pub relaxed, everyone suddenly aware of the silence.

'I'll have a pint of Guinness,' I said nervously, unsure of the correct manner in which to ask, knowing instinctively that such requests had their own familiar format.

She took a pint glass from beneath the bar. She slowly brought it close to the tap and placed it underneath at a forty-five degree angle to the bar. She pulled the tap and a brown liquid, accompanied by a coarse gushing sound, filled the glass.

She interrupted the procedure three-quarters of the way through and placed the nearly-full glass on a black plastic tray beside the taps.

I watched as the pint glass came to life, giving birth to true perfection. Waves pushed downwards, settling at ever-increasing heights, changing colour with each passing wave, until finally the two-toned mystery materialised – black covered by white.

I looked at my barmaid, forcing eye contact as my virginal mouth watered and my eyes beckoned her towards completion. She left her position of surveillance and came once again to the taps, taking what was soon to be mine in her hand and reintroducing it to the controlled flow of porter as she pulled the tap towards her.

Once again the brown liquid rushed forth, deep into the dark abyss below, mingling comfortably as the white purity rose towards the brim of the glass. The glass full, she once again placed it on the black tray, signalling to me that ownership was not yet mine. The new continued to meet with the old, integrating easily as the liquid darkness became complete. My barmaid stood guard, as I, helpless, looked on. Suspense thrilling – the wait killing.

Once again, for a final time it seemed, the full – almost over-full – glass was removed from the tray, cradled in the capable hands of the barmaid. She brought it to the tap, this time held straight, pushed the tap backwards rather than forwards, and once more the brown entered the black, and the white head over-flowed, sliding down the outside of the glass in a slow relaxed motion, like lava gently flowing down the outside of a crater.

The blackness glistened. The head, smaller now, sat proudly in place, and I marvelled at the beauty of it. The barmaid took her towel and wiped the excess from the glass, then, almost hur-ried, she placed the pint before me. All that was now required was to exchange money and at last I would gain possession of the coveted pint.

I placed my entire monetary possessions on the counter, beside my soon-to-possess pint. In a manner which seemed to pay reverence to the importance of the occasion, the barmaid took the ten-pound note by forefinger and thumb and silently mouthed 'thank you' with an elaborate movement of her lips.

I could wait no longer. I took the pint in my hand, raised it before me like the chalice of Christ, studied it, admired it, almost paid homage to it. The time had come. I brought the pint to my lips, slowly I pursed them, and craned my neck to meet my ris-ing arm. We touched, we entered. Slowly my arm rose, my neck withdrew, the instinct of nature taking over.

The Guinness flowed inward, going into my mouth, then my throat, easily. Slowly, like velvet it flowed, back and down, everywhere acknowledging its arrival, my eyes bulging to herald its coming.

The climax complete, I placed the glass once more before me. Half remained outside, half within. My virginity was gone. I had crossed the line from boy to man. I had entered a world unknown, a world of former whispers and wonder. I was free.

'Jesus, you were thirsty,' the voice of my barmaid said. I looked at her and back at my pint, and I smiled a broad smile of satisfaction.

'A long wait,' I replied, 'and worth it.'

'Will I start another or are you letting that sit awhile?' she asked.

'No,' I said, 'start away.' I picked up my pint once more, smiled, and asked myself what had taken me so long.

Satisfaction

Everything seemed different. I felt different. I felt light, as if I could float inches above the ground.

The people – the slaves – were growing heads at an alarming rate. The heads were moving in circles and some were even looking at me. I told them in my own mind to feck off and then the picture on the wall started moving. I looked in the mirror behind the bar to see if I was moving. I was going faster than everyone else.

I looked at the bar and saw my change. My hand tried to pick up the coins, but they too were moving. I wondered what was happening and struggled to regain control. Something was rising inside me and I fought to keep it back. It subsided, reluctantly, but I knew not for long.

The barmaid was coming closer. She looked bewildered and all her heads moved in a power-assuming fashion.

Success! My hand found my change. I gathered it together and put it in my pocket, deciding it was best to leave my hand there as well. I turned away from the bar and faced the door that I had entered earlier.

The daylight beckoned me, blinding my descent from the high stool. I stumbled, stretching out my empty hand to guard me from danger. I recovered and decided to stay still until the waving motion settled. I sensed a presence and heard someone ask me if I was okay, but I didn't answer.

The barmaid's voice rang in my ear, asking me how long I had waited. Answering herself she shouted, 'All your fucking life, you young bastard,' but I didn't care, I just wanted to go, to be on my own in a corner somewhere, anywhere.

I decided to make for the door. I ran at it, hoping my aim was good, and it was. I was out and away, and told never to return. I turned right and made my way towards the old market that is now a park, secluded from the street and protected by the river.

I stumbled on, happy, careless and free. I hummed a song of Ireland and wished I knew the words so I could sing it. I made plans for my future in my head and laughed at my persecutors. I crossed the street, oblivious to the beeping of car horns and shouted abuse. The gates of the park loomed near, the solitude of a bench enticing me. I stumbled on, arms outstretched, and the words of 'Seán South of Garryowen' came roaring out in some incomprehensible rush as I passed through to the safety of the park.

I sat slumped on a bench, aware that I was dribbling, my neck flopping, unable to control it. My stomach lurched, my body heaved and the sick gushed forth onto the bright green grass. Soon I was empty but still retching.

I struggled to regain control. The river was rushing past and I lay on a bench to listen to its peace. The sickness had passed and I moaned with exhaustion. I closed my eyes and fell asleep.

Wetness

Raindrops were beating off my face, my clothes were damp, but my jeans were wet. The taste in my mouth was foul and probably smelt like sewage. An unfamiliar pain banged in my head. I started to shake and fear took hold. I felt the urgency to move and I was crying inside.

I had felt fear many times before, like on the occasions I had waited for six-thirty and my father's return. My brother, the elder one, would smirk and pass me in silence, his report formulated and its delivery imminent. Gripped by fear, I used to look for somewhere to hide and find nowhere. I'd pray a silent prayer to the dead for help, for intervention, but it never came. The lights of my father's car would appear and fear would turn to panic as the punishment loomed near. My hands would cover my face and my bladder would leak, all control lost. The door would open, dialogue followed, and my name would be screeched as a stampede to find me ensued. The big frame towering above, my eyes pleading for mercy, my body shaking. His big hands would catch me and raise me above my own height, my back to the wall, as thumps were delivered in unforgiving frequency. Instructions to behave rang in my ears. Finally, his hand gone, I would drop, defeated in spirit, the travesty complete and my belief in justice gone. I used to silently scream in anger, bewilderment and frustration, but no sound came. The look on my face was the only expression of what was going on in my mind.

I got off the bench gripped in fear and the river beckoned. I remembered the sense of freedom I had felt, as I lifted the pint to my lips, the careless oblivion that ensued, and I yearned for its return. I tore my gaze from the river and walked to the gates of the park, my legs stiff and slighlty apart to separate my skin from the wetness of my trousers. My hand searched through my hair trying to discover the source of the pain.

I was wet, dirty and dishevelled and night was falling. Someone was looking at me, their eyes penetrating, and I wanted to run; all my courage was gone. I walked slowly and deliberately, exercising caution, my head feverish.

Gripped by my new fear I passed through the gates and joined the path and the people walking there. I fell in with them, walking faster, my destination unknown, finding safety in motion. People were looking at me. I saw them whisper and nudge each other as a squad car passed. I squealed in fear and broke into a trot, needing to get away, away from my crime, whatever that crime was.

I crossed the bridge onto a quieter road – where there were more cars and less people – hugging the wall as I went. As I neared home the fear subsided and I began to trust in the goodness of God, swearing to repent. I condemned the drink and swore abstinence. My acknowledgement of my wrong made me feel better, and I planned my re-entry to home.

I needed to change my clothes, hide what I was wearing and wash myself clean of any lingering odours. I bargained with God for a clear and unimpeded passage from the door to the bedroom and onwards towards the bathroom. Daily mass was promised, along with weekly confession and acts of charity, as the old familiar fear returned.

The house stood before me, sunk in the terrace, covered in darkness. I studied the door and reviewed my plans. If I was stopped I needed to hurl abuse and run for dear life, hoping to conceal my condition. I steadied my fear, breathing deeply. I told myself that there would be time to shiver, but now was the time to be firm.

Carefully I put my key in the lock, turned it and went in, closing the door quickly behind me. The room was dark and cold, smelling of must induced by dampness. It had recently been converted from its former function as a garage. Another door presented itself in the blackness, on the other side of which lay a narrow channel, a door leading off to another room and then the door to freedom. The channel led into the kitchen, where my brother would be, and the door off led to the dining-room, where my sister and mother would be. It was a short journey, but a perilous one, the obstacles fierce. I clenched my fists, breathed deeply once more and prayed to my grandmother.

I opened the door. My brother stared. I ran through, turning left. My mother stared and my sister smiled. I reached the final door. No one had moved. I reached the opposite side and saw the stairs before me, by the unused main entrance.

I bolted forwards, grabbing the banister, and took the steps two at a time. At the top three doors stood open; a fourth, to my parents' room, was locked. I went into my room and hurriedly stripped, looking for somewhere to hide the soiled garments of sin. I pushed the wardrobe forward and uncovered the false bottom underneath, quickly pushing in my jeans and jumper to where they would remain for ever.

Wearing nothing, I went back to the landing, where the hot press housed fresh underwear and household linen and towels. Complacency was setting in and I was slowing down. I told myself to hurry, the plan was working.

I grabbed a towel and clean socks and jocks and made for the bathroom. Once inside, I locked the door and, as the bolt crossed, my body relaxed. Immediately my head began to hurt again and the fear returned.

A Loving God

Life had changed, changed for ever. That dark hole of impending doom was no more. It was replaced with hope, happiness and, ultimately, escape. Everything became bearable. Anger replaced fear and I began to fight back, gaining belief in my worth and a growing confidence in my abilities.

I no longer waited on my father's six-thirty arrival. I was out exploring my world, mixing with the socially acceptable and scoring a few drinks. The effect was always the same. I gained release from my feelings, the urgency vanished and contentment reigned. When thoughts of home surfaced, the self-pity and anger returned, only to be dispelled once more by the arrival of yet another drink.

In the final year of school, my peers deliberated on their lives and careers. They fretted, their parents worried and the teachers advised. College was the topic of all conversation, interrupted occasionally by sex. I listened, rarely passed comment, pitied the fools and hated the smart ones. I wasn't going to college. Nothing attracted me about it. I knew what I wanted and college didn't have it.

I had decided that the Church could be useful. The clergy were revered, beyond reproach. I spoke to a priest, and then to another. I investigated their profession and the requirements to qualify. The results were encouraging. Success in the Leaving Cert. was desirable, but not essential. A belief in God and reverence to his Church was expected. Sexual stability was a requirement, while celibacy could be dealt with later. I qualified and my decision was made.

Most weekends I was to be found travelling towards the capital and the head house of many a religious order. My peers were to be found in hot pursuit of their co-ed females, hoping for intimacy against a backdrop of homosexual pop stars singing their latest hits. At least I had something in common with my fellows – we were all trying to get satisfaction while listening to homosexuals.

The headquarters of all religious were essentially the same. For me it was simply a matter of choice – who afforded the greatest freedom, and who was most tolerant in matters of alcohol. Drink, in varying forms, was available in all. Sometimes wine took precedence, while others opted for spirits. Porter was my preference, seconded by lager. I drank in them all, and got drunk in them all.

I listened to priests masturbating in the dark, while novices visited one another on the pretence of prayer. The nocturnal movements of the monastery would continue till morning, when, joined in prayer, they would forgive each other their sins and start a fresh day as God's servants.

I watched in awe but never inquired or questioned. I went unnoticed, drinking according to my needs, as my hosts busied themselves with protecting their secrets. They came to believe that, in me, they had found a true vocation.

I chose the Dominicans. They were the best, or, if you wish, the worst. They were a willing audience to which I had no difficulty in playing. Their structure was the most accommodating. They believed in a transitional period between leaving school and starting theological study, a time for maturing. A home was provided, meals were supplied, laundry taken care of and a communal car was available. The country was in depression. 250,000 were unemployed, but a year in the workforce – supported by the order while living together, learning to live as a community and pooling resources – was the recommended induction for all aspiring new members.

I loved it. There was no possible way I could get a job. I could spend all day searching, with money in my pocket, living in the capital away from home and sampling power whenever the opportunity arose. How could I go wrong?

As if that were not enough, the balance of power would shift at home. I would be respected, beyond reproach and impossible to question. The Church had power, and I would be part of that power. I made my intentions known, announcing my piety to all. My parents were overjoyed, my grandfather thrilled and the remainder nodded in approval. My brother, however, was shocked. My status was elevated, while his was diminished.

I could do what I liked and my life moved into the fast track. I was welcomed in pubs, encouraged by all. Drinks were invariably sent over and I toasted the goodness of God.
The money rolled in. The elders came first, their contributions large, in the hope of gaining an indulgence and with it eternal salvation. Then came the aunts, followed by the uncles. Some of it came in cards, wishing me well and requesting a prayer. Some came in cheques, with notes attached advising investment and, with all accruing interest – a prayer for the sender.

The old and infirm, poor and destitute all contributed, whispering thanks for my goodness in stopping. I promised them prayers and assured them of a place in heaven in the shadow of God himself.

Puberty Complete

My size increased. My belly got big, my chest broadened and my face bloated. The more I drank, the more I could drink. I was a regular in the pub, my custom valued. Fear was no more and even anger was at bay. The hangovers were mild and at times were pleasant. I had money in my pocket and the world was my oyster. I had the respect of my peers, the approval of my elders, the gratitude of my clergy and the tolerance of my family. I had it all, and no end was in sight. I called for a pint and I smiled.

The need to drink was constant. Nightly I craved it, and nightly I drank. The money kept coming and the drink kept flowing. My tolerance increased and I drank with men, never failing, never falling. The memory of that first time I cast aside, only to be recalled when advising a newcomer.

I conversed freely, regardless of the subject. I amended my vocabulary to suit my station, and I earned respect as a man of knowledge, character and spirit. I kept in regular contact with my future brothers in Christ, visiting them regularly both locally and in Dublin. I quickly became one of them and moved freely among them. They encouraged my studies and advised on exams. Plans were laid for my migration to them.

I met with others in my situation and humoured their calling to the service of Christ. We were greeted warmly, entertained pleasurably and fed gloriously. We attended mass and daily prayers, and my fellow aspirants seemed willing and genuine. When night came and the house fell silent, save for the groans and screams of a few, I made my way downwards to the cellars, where wine was in abundance and a rocking-chair supplied. My drinking would commence and comfort would come bringing with it scorn for some and pity for all.

On Sundays I journeyed home, maintaining a dignified bearing and protecting my motives. My arrival home was always sober, my face pious, my conversation easy and my attitude peaceful. I played on their guilt and escaped their pressure, relating elaborate tales of various missions of mercy.

Once free, I ran to the pub, greeted my friends, called a pint, lit a fag and delighted in my brilliance. The Guinness flowed softly, like velvet over velvet, down to the pit of my soul and life began again.

Adventures

Success in one endeavour often leads to arrogance in another. A one-time drinking buddy of mine was a great soccer player. He was also a great drinker. He used to get a glint in his eye whenever he scored a goal, and he got the same glint when he was heading for the pub. He was a master of public house rhetoric and radiated confidence.

However, he was doubly successful – I wasn't. He was lucky, he believed he was great before he started drinking. I had to have the drink before I came to the same belief.

I remember one occasion, when celebrating my imminent departure for Dublin, capital of Ireland and gateway to the world, we went to a pub where we were virtual unknowns. I was nervous, quiet, my guard well up and ready for fight. The other patrons, as well as the proprietors, exuded self-importance and were all well dressed. Brand names, important at the time, jumped off their pullovers, jeans and footwear, and they all had the same drink in front of them from the time they arrived until the time they left. In order to deal with the intimidation I felt, I called them all assholes and such like; in my head of course, for outwardly I just whispered and most times no words came.

My friend was the opposite. He went in roaring, slapping, punching, doing a shadow box and screaming for porter. Everyone knew him. His fame had travelled the two miles and his skill on the field was renowned. I called for two pints and they duly arrived. I sat at the bar in a semi-foetal position. My eyes were fixed on the floor and my right hand held my pint for security. My friend was by this time running from person to person, abusing them all, for he was the greatest. He was spilling his drink as if he were a million-aire, though still sober, and I was sweating.

I called him to come and join me, but he ignored me. I began to think that everyone was looking at me and that I was the source of their laughter. They were probably saying that I was a retard, and an ugly one at that, playing lapdog to sanctity and being its servant when required. The more they laughed, the more he shouted. My eyes stayed fixed on the ground and the sweat dripped from me. They were all talking about me, sneering, calling me a gayboy, and then the shakes came. I couldn't hear them, but I knew.

I still had some of my pint left and couldn't leave without drinking it. The door, just ten feet away, seemed a long way off. They were saying worse things now. My mouth was dry and my face hot. I grabbed my pint, slightly reassured that it was there, and held it for dear life.

I planned my escape. I decided to wait until they were divert-ed by the telly, when they would look away. Unseen, I'd drink my pint and invisibly make for the door. Once outside, I'd turn left and walk fast around the corner, to another pub.

I waited and waited. I started to get angry and to hate them all. I picked out one or two, including my friend, and I decided to hate them the most. They were the ones I would get. I invented imaginary friends in the Mafia to whom I'd give the contract. Upon hearing my story they'd take out these bastards, accepting no fee, glad to remove such scum from the world.

The sports results came up on the television. All eyes turned. Now was my chance. I clenched my fists, bolted for the door, burst through into the street and ran as fast as I could.

Departure

It was time, in the eyes of all, to become a man of God – only I knew the truth. The train to Dublin, the bus to Dominic Street, the shake of a hand and I was now a Dominican.

Our house in Glasnevin wouldn't be ready for weeks. The builders were on a go-slow, or else the money was. I think, myself, it was the money. We were installed in an orphanage, as a temporary measure, and told to be positive, that the experience would do us good.

There were seven of us in all. We varied in age. Four of us were young, fresh from school. The others were seasoned, in their twenties, and probably hiding. I was escaping, so that was OK. The priest in charge was young, as priests go. He was the ambitious type, the sort of man who, if encountered in the business world, would have been known as a 'dangerous bastard' – he'd definitely take no prisoners. It became apparent, too, that he was always assessing and reassessing.

We were placed in cubicles which had formerly been occupied by inmates, and mine overlooked the street. My first night as a man of God was spent sitting on my windowsill watching the drug dealers and prostitutes doing their business in the street below. I thought it best to refrain from going for a pint, at least until I had found my feet and knew the run of the place. It was hard to resist, but I managed anyway.

To my amazement, all but one of my fellow holy men had arranged employment for themselves. One lad was going to work in a cash and carry – his father had arranged it – while another was truly holy and was already working in the Catholic Information Office on O'Connell Street. Everyone had, it seemed, procured employment as a direct result of either the Church or their parents. This took the pressure off me to find gainful employment, as, being a proud man, I would refuse any intervention, settling only for what I could achieve myself. And, with the amount of people on the dole, there wasn't much hope of finding anything.

I was seventeen years old, as green as grass, with no experience and no skills. I had worked as a floor boy in two different hotels, collecting glasses and robbing as much change as possible, pretending it was gratuities. The Americans were the only ones that ever actually tipped. My fellow Irishman believes he pays enough in the retail price to mark his gratitude.

I was now expected to walk the streets of Dublin, asking for work, from nine to five with weekends off. It was typical of the Church. They were and are so far removed from reality with their heads tightly tucked up their own arses that they actually believed it would be possible for me to march into the job of the century. I am the ambitious type, but ambition and drive had nothing to do with it. Some distant and aloof theologian had decided that this was the way to ensure that only genuine vocations got through. The process was intended to deter all the child abusers, sex perverts and closet homosexuals from ending up as ordained ministers of Christ. In fact it made it easier, of course. All the freedom in the world was available. Even the priest in charge was said to be shagging a nun. I thought this was hilarious – and ambition took a holiday!

University

On my first day as an aspiring priest I went on the piss. The day started in the 'Parnell Mooney' at the end of the street where I had seen all the drug pushers and prostitutes.

The Guinness in Dublin tasted different, more solid, and colder. It was quite nice and I decided that I could get used to it – with practice. The bar men were different too. The ones at home resembled bank managers. They were slow, quiet and very aloof. They always maintained a respectful distance from the customer, while keeping one eye on the till and one eye on the said customer. I had watched them many times, dispensing booze and collecting money. The money came first – no money, no drink – even if you had parted with everything you had in the world to their benefit. I had placed the one I disliked most on my hit list, to be taken out at a later date by either the IRA or the Mafia. I quite liked Colonel Gadaffi as well, but his buckos would stand out too much in Ireland.

The Dublin barman was a salesman who occasionally became a philosopher. He was adept at conversing on any known subject, and he always knew a man, that knew a man, that knew the man. There was more to be learned from that Dublin barman than there was from all the professors in Trinity. He was there for the money, but he didn't make it obvious. He welcomed all sorts, although, like everyone, he hated sleepers, especially in the toilets. By and large the Dublin barmen were a nicer bunch, who knew life was tough and were used to insecurity. They didn't understand possession, unlike their country brothers, who were still too close to the land and a sense of ownership. I owned nothing and saw no merit in associating with those that did.

I walked up O'Connell Street, having left the 'Parnell' slightly steamed. People were hurrying, cars were racing and buses roaring. I didn't care, I was feeling no pain. I crossed the street, a dangerous mission at any time, and decided to investigate a side street. To my delight I found another Mooney's, this time the 'Abbey Mooney' – a longer bar, with peculiar walls of moulded vegetation – and my education continued.

The rest of the day is a blur, a hazy memory of uncertain facts. I remember beans on toast, a cup of coffee, the heads of the six postulants, a priest, all behaving strangely as I knelt in prayer beside the holy toilet bowl calling on God and anyone else that could help.

My brothers in Christ weren't too impressed. They were all too holy and in love with the one true Church to condone my behaviour. I had soon distanced myself from half of them, having decided with good reason that these were gay and really only wanted varying degrees of perverted sexual gratification. There was one in particular who was so sexually twisted that I genuinely believe he had the makings of a serial child abuser – and the Dominican fathers loved him. The other three weren't as bad; in fact I never figured out why they had joined. They were definitely running from something – looking for a way out.

I was 'spoken to' after my day on the piss. It wasn't on – I'd have to give the drink a miss on weekdays. This was communicated to me by our spiritual adviser, alias the priest in charge. This man was in his mid-thirties and he was, in effect, telling a seventeen-year-old that it was OK to drink, even though the legal age was eighteen. Clearly the law didn't apply to the Roman Catholic Church and I was part of that Church.

A priest in the nearby friary died. The friary was up the street from the orphanage, and this priest had been loved by all the inmates past and present. Despite not having known him I was told to attend his funeral, and Robbie, a fellow postulant from the six counties, was to accompany me. I didn't mind because I had nothing else to do anyway and I had run out of money. There was to be a party afterwards and, knowing the holy fathers, that meant there would be drink as well. The priest in charge of us slept in the priory – he felt the orphanage was too spiritual for him – so it would also give me a chance to see where he hung out.

Robbie was a gem. He was young and strong and loved the birds. If he wasn't so young I'd have said he was running away from the RUC or a punishment gang or such like. He certainly wasn't there out of conviction and an unshakeable love of Christ. He had many stories to tell. The British soldiers used to set up their campfire on his front lawn. In fact, his sisters were almost raped by the English filth.

The Dominicans had a history of supporting rebels. Indeed, in my native town they were the only ones that allowed the IRA into their church during the war of independence and afterwards. To this day an annual mass commemorating the 1916 rising takes place in the Dominican church. Imperial lovers like the Redemptorists excommunicated the freedom fighters and wouldn't give them the sacraments. That is when the Church began to lose its grip, I believe. At the back of it all we are Druids with common sense. The ground we live on is our God – we are the purest breed of nationalists that can be found anywhere in the world. The Church took sides. They took the wrong side. I think that my tolerance of the Dominicans came from the knowledge that they too, in some small way, believed in freedom.

At heart I am a rebel. I believe in Ireland and the Irish. I have a great sense of what it means to be Irish. I sat as a child in the kitchen in my ancestral home in north Cork and listened to my grandfather talk of the land and the strength that was in it. I listened to my grand-uncle, the retired village master, telling of his experiences with the Black and Tans and the RIC. I heard of emigration, and starvation and poverty so dire that my belly ached. I listened to the ramblers, *an bohántaíocht*, telling of their part in the fight to free Ireland and the bitterness that followed. I loved them all and I was proud to be one of them. They were the great men, the men that built my Ireland, and to have a true sense of Ireland a man must first have a sense of those men. I lived among them and I loved them deeply. My grandfather was the greatest man I have ever known, and I have known a few.

People confuse the love of the land with ownership of it. Ownership has nothing to do with it. It's about belonging, it's about respect. I don't own any land in the conventional way, but I belong to much of it. I belong because it is my birthright to belong. I belong to the people that work the land and they belong to me. It took me years and a lot of loneliness to discover this. The great man, my grandfather, had to die in order for me to return and I will never again leave. I will never again be made to leave. Ireland is in my heart, and my sense of place comes from my home and my people. My forefathers fought and died so that I could belong. They didn't do so in vain.

The Church was full of priests. Robbie and I sat and watched as the pomp and ceremony of the funeral mass took place unashamedly in a poverty-stricken parish in the inner city. I didn't take much notice of the service. I was only there because I had to be. Afterwards we went into the back for the social part of the proceedings, but I was seriously disappointed with the spread and I decided to leave. It was September and Ireland was enjoying an Indian summer. I decided that I'd head off to St. Stephen's Green, in the hope of seeing a good number of scantily-clad women. I asked Robbie if he wanted to join me and – shock, horror – my brother in Christ said he would.

The green was fabulous. Girls of all ages lay on the grass wearing bras with the straps hanging loosely down their arms. The view was amazing.

'You boys are clerical students, are you not?' I heard someone say from behind. I looked round and saw a man in his mid-thirties wearing a sandy beard, a green tweed jacket and a pair of Jesus sandals. 'I saw you at the funeral this morning,' he continued, easing the awkwardness. 'Dominicans are you?'

'Yes,' I said, 'that's right, and you?'

'I'm diocesan, out on a break, trying to make up my mind,' he informed us.

'You were very quick to spot us,' said Robbie, his streetwise northern senses sharpening.

'We clerics spot each other,' he replied. I could smell the shit, but I was in no position to dismiss even the most dubious diversion. 'Fancy a coffee, or maybe something stronger?' he asked, the diversion improving.

'Sure,' I said, 'but we don't have any money.'

'Ah, that doesn't matter, I'm buying. Billy is the name, by the way. What's yours?'

We introduced ourselves as we left the green heading for a pub. Billy was a great character. He knew all the angles and he had loads of money. We drank the afternoon away and I had more pints than Robbie because I was able to drink more and faster. I got pissed and Robbie took me home. Billy said he'd call the next day with a book he thought I should read. I hoped he would, because I knew I'd need a cure.

Billy called the next day and every other day after that. Robbie said he was a sleazeball and he wanted nothing to do with him. I knew that there was something about him, but I didn't delve too deeply. He was buying the liquor, and meals as well. I opened my heart and told him all about home and the way I was reared. It was a great hard luck story, of course, but I thought that the more sorrow he felt for me the nicer he would be. All I wanted was the piss-up and I would tell him anything in order to get it.

I was very impressionable, of course. Billy spoke about bish-ops and influential friends. He told me that a friend of his was a bishop in the midlands and that all I had to do was say the word and I could leave the Doms, who I had just joined, and become a diocesan student like him. His friend the bishop would be only too glad to have me. Something told me, however, that it was my arse the bishop wanted and not my soul.

The piss-up continued. I was lucky that I had an immense capacity for Guinness, as I could drink all day and all night and still know what I was doing. I never got drunk in the fall-down type of way. It must have cost Billy a fortune, but he played and lost. I played and won – in the way I wanted to win that is, for if I had really won I wouldn't have been anywhere near Billy or any of the other bastards in the first place.

Disease

After a month the money ran out. It must have, because Billy disappeared. I went on the dry and then I got sick. My immunity was shattered from a month on the booze.

I was lucky, I had a chronic disease as well. My asthma provided me with a cover. The priest in charge decided to transfer me to the safety of Tallaght, the head house, where conditions were warmer and the air drier. In hindsight I think my illness provided the priest with an opportunity to face up to his responsibilities. He had known about Billy, because Robbie had grassed on me. To my mind, this also explained what Robbie was doing in the Doms – either he or one of his family were grassing on the IRA and he had run away to Dublin to save himself from their wrath. It was a good theory and I liked it. It justified my growing hatred of the prick.

I was given a room on the third floor, beside the main exit, a situation I specifically requested in order to allow my forthcoming nocturnal activities to pass unnoticed. It was a grand room with a soft bed and a wardrobe. There was a sink also, and that doubled as a piss-pot when I woke at five in the morning. I was given a key to the main door, so I could go for a walk in the fresh air, whenever I needed, to help me breathe. I was glad to have the key, because I was able to slip out for a fag and slip back in again and no one was any the wiser.

There were twenty bedrooms on my floor, but only four were occupied. I found out who my neighbours were and decided to keep my door locked, because one of them had a reputation. I was very naïve. Anyone could have spotted that the Doms, and indeed the Church at large, was struggling for survival. Priests were leaving like flies. I thought at the time it was because they had become too fond of the good life and had found women they couldn't resist. However, I now believe that all the good ones were leaving because they couldn't tolerate the bad ones.

Because I was sick with my chest and wasn't getting better, I was exempt from prayers in the morning and allowed to rest till midday. If I thought my chest was improving I stopped taking my tablets for a day or two and, once my condition worsened and my breathing became laboured again, my morning lie-in wasn't threatened.

Money was sent from home once or twice and, though not a lot, it still helped to allow me to sit sipping Guinness in the 'Fox's Covert' across the road on a couple of occasions. I found the keys to the offertory boxes in the church and was appalled when I discovered that most of the boxes contained nothing more than coppers. Still, altogether they made up a few quid and over to the 'Fox's' I went.

The paltry contributions from home, together with my raids on the offertory boxes, still didn't make enough for a good piss-up. The only money lying about was in the boxes, so any other hopes of getting my hands on decent cash were fairly dim. I could, however, get started with a pint in the 'Fox's' and then return to the room near the kitchen where all the home-made wine was kept. I called this my cellar. The wine was contained in tubular bottles and varied in potency. Some nights I got pissed in no time, while others I could be drinking until morning and I still wouldn't be drunk.

It's a dangerous thing to drink alone. The mind has nothing to occupy it and is constantly throwing up ideas to entertain the solitary man, or in my case the solitary boy. It takes great discipline to reject the majority of these ideas and, I admit, I sometimes succumbed. The simplest tasks, sober, can be the most difficult ones when drunk. I was sitting in my cellar one night and, having consumed a couple of bottles of wine to wash down the seven or eight pints I had had earlier, I decided that I was hungry.

The cook normally put leftover meals on plates in a warming trolley. I went to the kitchen and found the trolley full of plates covered in tin foil –.roast pork, accompanied by broccoli, carrots and lovely potatoes, but stone cold. I placed a dinner on the gas ring and lit it. A couple of minutes later I heard a bang and found that the plate had cracked in four and was lying under the ring in bits. I got another dinner from the trolley and once again placed it on the ring, sure that the previous plate had been faulty. I heard a bang again. I placed two more plates on the ring and the same thing happened as before. I was disgusted with the kitchen staff. The quality of their plates was disgraceful.

I commenced the tidy up and put my hand under the ring to pick out a piece of broken plate. The tips of my fingers were cut by the razor-sharp edges and blood flowed. I decided to leave the mess. First thing in the morning I would report the matter to the provincial in charge and request him to conduct an inquiry to ascertain who had purchased the plates and cheated the Dominicans out of good quality delph that could withstand the heat of a flaming gas ring. I turned out the lights and stumbled off to bed.

I woke the following morning at ten o'clock and decided to stay in bed, as my chest had been very bad all night. I was lucky to have made it. Some of my fingers were even bleeding. I was very sick, very sick indeed.

Inquiries

Every house, except a flat-roofed house, has an attic. Attics are great places, full of stuff that was once important and has been kept for memories. Some attics are now being converted to make rooms, or gyms. I think it a shame, for where will the memories go?

The religious house that I lived in was no different, except that it was possible to walk through the attic without falling through to the room below. I often spent my afternoons in the attic searching through boxes, some with names, others with none. The possibility of finding something worth selling was very high and no better boy than me to sell it. I found a couple of things, like a dart board for which I got five pounds from a street trader, but I never found anything of any real significance.

One afternoon I had come across a number of Dominican habits and priestly collars. I tried them all on and decided to keep the best, just for the craic. It was well I did.

I spent my days in Tallaght roaming around and talking to people, some of whom were very interesting. I was walking in the garden one day when I saw a man praying, with the hood of his holy habit pulled over his face. I sat down beside him and I spoke to him in a very simple way for the most of the afternoon. His name was Father William and he was extremely gentle and had a great appreciation for nature. I later discovered that he was in fact the deposed Archbishop of Iran. The Ayatollah had thrown him out when he seized power. I like to think that in this man I met a truly holy one. He was definitely a man of God and humility was an integral part of his character. I met a man years later who had been gone from the priesthood for more than thirty years. He had been ordained in the fifties, at the height of the Church's reign, and had travelled and studied in his native Scotland, in France and Rome. He told me that, in all, he had only ever met three truly holy men. I met only one, so between us we had met four.

I was summoned by the director of vocations one morning and I arrived late, just to prove that I was still sick. He asked me lots of questions about my activities and wanted to know how I was spending my time, having no formal programme to follow. I told him what he wanted to hear, and he seemed happy to think that I was spending my time meditating on the temptations of Christ. Anyway, they were desperate and needed every vocation they could get. This was about survival.

I did such a good job in selling him the meditation bullshit that I forgot to wheeze and, when I had finished ranting on like a guilty convict faced with solitary confinement, he told me that I was going back to the orphanage the following day. I was glad; the monastery was getting too stuffy anyway. The only thing I'd miss would be the wine.

I packed my bags that night and decided to go easy on the drink, as I needed to be in good shape for my return to my brothers in Christ. I went to the cellar at ten, as usual, poured myself a little drink and sat down on my rocking-chair to ponder my predicament. I was glad to be leaving, but would need money, and I had none. No mon, no fun. I rocked away, having a drink, back to the wall and heading for the corner. Then it came to me, the greatest plan of all.

Money

The pro-cathedral, just off Dublin's main street, is always busy with a regular flow of all types of people. A lot of devout country people, in Dublin for the day, make a point of stopping to say a prayer.

Elderly people love the priest. He is God's representative. In fact, to some he is God. The priest is their ticket to heaven. His prayers, his direct intercessions with God, especially during the mass, will guarantee the worst sinner entry to paradise and a bypass of St. Peter. Unfortunately, or fortunately I should say, everything has its price. Even the priest has his. To say a mass for a sinner, the dead or the ill costs money.

I decided that my discovery in the attic was my ticket to evenings of blissful happiness, drinking my favourite in its native town. Mass cards are an easy thing to acquire and in my case the stamper, as it was known, was easier still. During my lazy days in Tallaght I had sometimes been given responsibility for the front desk. On one of these occasions I slipped a stamper – a print of a priest's name – into my bulging pocket, and so completed my kit.

On my first morning back in the orphanage, to create a good impression, I left at an early hour, under the pretext of looking for a job. I went down to the pro-cathedral, armed with my priestly collar, mass cards and stamper, and proceeded to make lucrative sales, until enough was gathered for a good day's supping. I convinced myself that some day I'd be ordained and that I'd say the mass then, but it really didn't bother me – at least not until all the money was drunk and I was broke once more.

When one wears the priestly garb all sorts of people are attracted to you. In pubs, washed-up alcoholics of an earlier generation always pester the priest. I didn't mind being pestered – that has a price as well. I was bought a good number of pints while listening to the innocent confessions of my fellow drinkers as we occupied the snugs of many a public house. I did everything bar say mass, but given the opportunity . . . !

The Dark Side

You meet strange people in pubs and I have met my share. There is always somebody smarter, someone who has been where you are and is ready to exploit you. If I had money I didn't need to be with anyone – I just drank alone. Money meant security. The danger was when the money was going or gone.

The craving for drink is a powerful thing. It's the only thing I know that can completely bollox a man. I heard of a man once who took off his shoes and sold them for drink, he was that desperate. Another fellow let a homosexual interfere with him for the price of twenty pints. When a man reaches this level he has sold his soul, and a comeback is hard to imagine. It's not impossible, but as close as you can get. I never went that far, but I came close. The pubs of Dublin are full of scum, waiting and watching. Billy was one of those scumbags, but I played him well. You've got to think like a scumbag to beat a scumbag, and I'm a good thinker if feck all else. After my time in Tallaght I had come to realise that Billy had only been out for what he could get. I knew that he had probably been thrown out of the seminary, if indeed he was ever there at all.

I had been back with my group for about three weeks when I was caught with the habit I'd found in the attic. It was confiscated, but the priest in charge didn't take me to task. I don't think he had the balls.

I met up with Billy again and he seemed to have plenty of money. I knew he was looking for someone vulnerable, so I became that someone, as I had before. The liquor poured, the money too, and the game got dangerous. I was a wild thing, in from the wild, being spoon-fed and getting to like it. After a while the instincts of the wild relax.

The vultures circle while the lion sleeps.

The Dominicans didn't care. They were too busy dealing with their own problems to see the ones I was creating. They were supposed to be looking out for me, but they didn't even know I drank the way I did – either they couldn't see what was happening under their own noses or they chose to ignore it.

I drank to excess in the exalted company of my vulture. He was closing for a kill – and I mean a kill. It is most likely that he had an elaborate plan to enslave me, rape me, then kill me. By that time, though, I'd have been a drunken bum thrown out of the Dominicans, forgotten about, and no one would have missed me. My grave would have been a shallow one somewhere in the Dublin mountains, buried face down, my arse cocked for one last rub of my corpse before the clay sealed in his stinking semen.

I decided to run. Familiar faces, known locations and even my brother were better than that. I stopped the drinking, told Billy to fuck himself, controlled the craving, packed my bags, got to Houston and jumped on a train. I didn't turn around, for turning to salt had crossed my mind.

I was now an atheist, and everyone knew it. I had only one problem – I had no money and no one to ask for it. Most people were looking for refunds. I'd have loved to have told them that their money had mixed with the Liffey long since and had travelled to pollute the shores of England, therefore not being entirely wasted. I didn't of course, for a contribution towards the pollution of the Shannon would have been greatly appreciated.

Laughing and Crying

The brother was back on top, and I was lower than ever. The Dominicans had shown concern when it was too late and had enlightened my family. The brother loved it, the mother took valium, the father gave ultimatums. The honeymoon was over – I was back in the shit.

I got odd jobs and then went on the piss. The craving was back and wouldn't go away. It was no longer a requirement, pleasurably received to facilitate the continuation of sanity, but a crippling necessity that ruled the mind.

It went on for a year, never getting better, always worse. Respect was lost and a bad name earned. Yet, some took a chance and gave me a break. At times I earned good money and drank even more heavily, but the more I drank the harder it was for the pain to go away. I was digging a hole and covering it as well. Having no money was the worst thing that could happen. A day is a long time when you've no money. Sometimes I stayed in bed to kill the day. If I was lucky, I slept, and I was luckier still if, when I woke, I was tired from sleep and slept again. That day passed and the following one came. At least I was one day closer to getting the dole.

A conspiracy commenced, my brother its author. He was a bastard, and top of my hit list. My plans for him were the most dramatic. Gadaffi's boys would take him out, castrating him before death and feeding his balls to cats. They'd then stick his prick in his mouth, like the cocksucker he was. When he was dead, his body would be flown to Libya, made into horsefeed and sold for the equivalent of a bag of manure, and dispatched to feed the starving horses of the Sahara desert. Everyone would assume he had flipped and emigrated without a trace, leaving me to assume command. Once I was in control, drink would be legalised, parties thrown, my mother evicted, destined for the streets, and anyone that wanted to stay on would do so at their own peril.

My brother had the locks changed, and I had nowhere to go.

Sleeping rough is a difficult thing. It's not something you can just fall into, it needs to be planned. To find yourself unprepared for the situation can be very dangerous. It wouldn't have been as bad if it happened in the summer, but it happened to me in the dead of winter. However, any hardship worth enduring is worth enduring well.

I grew up in the age of the switch. Whatever you wanted you just flicked a switch and it happened. Hot water at the flick of a switch, followed by light, heat and entertainment. There are no light switches underneath a sycamore tree. Clothing is an important part of the rough sleeper's kit. A good coat can be rendered useless if the shirt beneath has been carelessly placed – next to the skin in the absence of a vest. Once the cold gets in it doesn't get out.

Cardboard boxes are an invaluable asset – good cardboard can make a great nest – but a dry place is essential. Underneath a bridge, if it is a modern bridge, is probably the best location and is much sought after. Garden sheds and abandoned houses all make for good accommodation, the only problem being that you're never sure when an interruption might take place. It often happens that the bastard that owns the shed in question checks his investment at two o'clock in the morning, and then you're fucked – cops and all.

Gathering my kit was easy. I called on my friend, Seán, and he helped. He didn't know he helped as much as he did. I didn't tell him I was sleeping rough, just that I was running away from home. Being quite familiar with my people, he didn't ask any questions. I have often wondered since why I didn't tell him or his parents. They were and are good people. His mother was always good to me – she was warm in a motherly kind of way. I know now that she would have helped had I asked her to, and I regret that I didn't.

Of all the physical and mental scars I have, the effects of sleeping rough are by far the worst. It's something I will never get over. For all the hard images it conjures in the minds of others, in me it conjures nothing but fear and shame. My soul cries in the dark every time I think of it or see something to remind me of it.

I walked out of a gentlemen's club in Dublin many years later, my boss at my side. As we came to the bottom of the steps, a rough sleeper was getting himself ready for the night. I started to sweat and my hands shook and I couldn't hear what my boss was saying. I put my hand in my pocket and silently withdrew a five-pound note. I let the note drop as I passed the rougher. I was trembling all over and fighting the desire to scream. The night-mares were back, but I was still awake. That night, I stayed in a plush hotel, but I couldn't sleep because I was afraid.

It's every man's right to have a roof over his head.

I know people now who have five and six houses. I also have one and a mobile home by the sea. Yet my fellows sleep rough, and in the dark I sleep with them and the fear of Jesus and every-thing he has grips me and I am scared. I can feel the cold and the rain and the hunger in my belly. I can hear the rats and the screams of sleeping drunks. I can see the world moving, unaware that I even exist.

51

I slept in a shed once. Although it was a garden shed, the wooden type, it was not in a garden. A mechanic who operated near my home used it as his tea room and it was thoughtfully equipped with a bench to sleep on and a table to eat from. It was abandoned each evening at six and never locked, for the only thing of value was the shed itself.

It got very cold one night and there was no switch. I tried to get warm, but the cold was in. All around me lay newspapers from the day's tea breaks, along with milk cartons and plastic bags. I opened my window to act as a chimney and, gathering my fuel, lit a fire. The shed filled with smoke – the chimney wasn't able to cope. The fire got bigger and a piece of wall joined in. I couldn't breathe and had to leave. I stood on the road and watched in horror as my home burned. The fire brigade came and I ran off.

When I sobered up I realised how stupid I'd been. I had lit fires under the new bridge, but it was concrete and only got black. No one interfered with me under there and, though miserable, it was a contented misery. I gathered a good kit, bit by bit, and even came by a few pairs of socks when passing a clothes-line one afternoon. The Lord always provides. I still got the dole, because I still had an address. Even if I hadn't, I'd have got one. There was always an address available for a small price.

Tuesday was dole day and I would eat like a lord and get pissed as a fart. The rest of the week I schemed and occasionally I begged. Charity was not an option. The St. Vincent de Paul were a shower of grab-all, take-all, give-fuck-all-back bastards.

I called one night at the scheduled time of 7.30. I was told to go to the waiting-room and someone would call me in due course. The room was big, situated at the front of a Georgian house. Chairs were placed in a circle in the middle of the floor. There were two other clients waiting to be dealt with and I sat with them, even though I didn't like the look of them.

One fellow was a known homo who gave blow-jobs to sick bastards on the river bank. What this piece of shit was doing in

52

the room was beyond me. The other client looked no better, added to which he was wearing white shoes, so I decided that they were probably lovers. I felt sick, but I had nothing to get sick with.

After a while the door opened and a do-gooder – the type who collects the money at mass on a Sunday and would piss in your eye half an hour later – walked in. He called the first man and beckoned him into a corner. Twenty pounds passed hands and a lot of whispering went on. I wondered was it an advance payment.

The known homo left and White Shoes was called to the corner. Another twenty pounds passed with less whispering. The do-gooder showed White Shoes to the door and they both went out. I was alone in the room and decided I'd investigate, to see if there was anything I could pocket for my kit. I walked to the window and, lo and behold, there were my two fucking steamers heading off up the street, all but holding hands.

The room was completely bare, there wasn't even a tea towel. I wondered where all the stuff was kept. I thought of the ads on the television looking for donations and felt sure that I'd soon have a roof over my head, if not a few quid as well. I waited for ages and then the do-gooder came back and told me that the man who dealt with new cases was busy and to call back in an hour.

I left the house and went for a walk around the town, hoping I might meet someone that I could tap for a few quid. It was night time so there weren't many around and when the hour was up I went back to the house. I was still hungry.

The new case man looked like a DIY type. He wore a brown jacket with a red sleeveless jumper underneath, like the type of fella you see working in hardware stores. He called me into the hallway and conducted his interview near the safety of the front door. He asked me what my difficulty was, and I told him that I was homeless, destitute, starving, cold, thinking of suicide and generally fucked. He nodded his head to everything I said and wore a condescending smile, which I imagine was supposed to signal empathy. When I was finished he took an envelope from his pocket, handed it to me and told me I'd be fine. He said that I was a fighter, that I was young and that he had great confidence in me. He showed me the door and quickly locked it behind me.

Back on the street, I was gobsmacked, my fantasy of a night in a bed shattered. I walked back towards the centre of town and, like playing the lottery, I was almost afraid to open my envelope. I kept moving to help me stay warm and wondered if the contents were going to feed me as well as get me pissed. I took the envelope from my pocket and slowly, deliberately, I opened it. I nearly fainted with the shock. Three pounds, three measly fucking pounds, was all that was there! I decided they had made a mistake and about-turned and hurried back to the St. V. de P. The door was locked when I arrived, so I banged as hard as I could to ensure I was heard. The two steamers had got forty quid between them and I, a genuine case, had only got three.

The door opened and the do-gooder stood there, all importance, wanting to know what it was I wanted. I told him about my three pounds and told him how desperate I was, making sure to have a desperate look on my face. He started to close the door and told me to come back when I was better behaved. I told him to go and fuck himself, and he told me he'd call the guards. I called him a pillow-biting puff and he slammed the door.

I walked away seething with anger and, remembering that the bastard would probably call the guards, I started to run. I was not going to hang around to be a punchbag for those bastards, thrown in a cell, and risk losing my place under the bridge as well.

The St. Vincent de Paul were now on my hit list, right at the top, sharing joint No. 1 with the brother. The only problem was that Hitler was dead and I'd have to allocate a suitable maniac to take them out at a later date.

Windows

If there is anything good at all to be said about sleeping rough, it is the freedom. I always craved freedom, and motion with it. The two combined create a great sense of security and can even bring peace of mind – though that is rare enough and is usually reserved for a belly full of porter or swimming in the sea.

I was never aggressive with drink, in fact I was quite the opposite. I always had a good capacity for booze; until the end, of course, when everyone's capacity is gone. I used to love that moment when, not yet pissed, but not sober either, the romance of Irish poets would fill my mind and it felt great to be alive. During that short-lived window of time the urgency of living, the battle to survive, the panic for the future and how I'd exist, all subsided and the feeling was the most beautiful I have ever known.

Quite uniquely, I also found this release – or window of peace – in an environment quite removed from alcohol. In a rocky cove off the west coast of Ireland the greatest swim in the world is to be found.

I am also a swimmer.

My family used to holiday near this cove on an annual basis, and many day trips were made. Strangely, even with money in my pocket, I'd forego a drink in favour of a swim.

The cove was quite dangerous and unsuitable for the weak and frail. It was therefore reserved for men, though this tradition was developed by the Christian Brothers and, with their reputation of recent years, I can only guess at what inspired them. A deep channel protected by submerged cliffs on either side led from the cove to the sea. On rough days the wave action in this channel was treacherous, acting like a suction pool into the ocean beyond.

I loved the rough days. The challenge was immense. The other men, lying naked on the rocks tanning their balls, would watch in horror as I made my way through the channel and, once clear, swim like crazy to my position just off the head. The ocean, unaware of my intrusion, continued to boil. I longed to be a fish. Lying on my back treading water, thoughts of the world left on shore, I could have stayed for ever, all fear gone, filled with peace. Eventually I'd have to give in to the cold, and immediately the spell was broken and the window was lost to me once again. I'd head for shore, battling the channel, and on reaching land the torment returned.

The winter was getting worse and, with it, my situation. My health was suffering, though my mind wasn't – at least, I didn't think it was. The asthma was a curse and the dampness was evil. I wasn't allowed into pubs anymore, because they said I was smelly. Drinking at home had never been my scene and, though my home was now the underneath of a bridge, I didn't drink there either. I needed the ambience of a pub and the presence of people in order to enjoy a pint. Drinking in the cellar in Tallaght was somehow different – it wasn't home, more like my private pub where my imaginary friends in drink resided.

I put my pride in my pocket and called on my father, begged for mercy, got it and left the streets behind. The mother went mad, the brother plain crazy. They insisted on conditions and the old man agreed. No drink and I stay, drink and I'm gone. I agreed: I had no choice.

Emigration

A warm bed, good food, hot water and my health soon returned. I kept the conditions, but the urgency was rising. Nothing so strong could stay buried for long. I decided to emigrate.

I got the boat and went to London. I had been saving my dole – through keeping the conditions – and the prospect of freedom returned. I arrived at Piccadilly Circus – not an acrobat in sight. Onwards towards the 'Elephant and Castle', thinking I'd see the Queen. I saw 'The Crown' instead. A pint of lager, a chat with a Brit, the pull of a fag and I had joined my countrymen in the development of the world.

I must have been a miserable sight as I walked to Charing Cross and boarded the train to my final destination. There I was, satchel in hand, wearing my bottle-green bomber jacket, economy-class jeans and a pair of well-worn runners. My face was bloated, my gut swollen and my arse was bleeding from the coarseness of lager, to which I was unaccustomed. I feared an assault and held my pocket. In hindsight, I was probably the more feared. It seemed there were no English left in England.

The place was full of Blacks, Chinese, Iraqis and some of Gadaffi's gang were there as well. I wondered if the IRA knew but decided they didn't, because they'd never have planted a bomb which could have killed some of our brothers in bondage.

I travelled south-east to Lee and my journey was complete. My aunt – my father's sister – met me, unaware of my nature and in for a shock. She liked the gin herself, so maybe she'd understand. My first night I decided to celebrate. I got pissed, told everyone I was over there on a job and finally fell asleep.

My aunt didn't know what to make of me. An energetic maniac had entered her house, breathing life into a coffin that wanted to stay closed. Life to her was a test of faith, it was never to be enjoyed. She sinned nightly, with a bottle of gin, searching for her own personal window. I think she saw herself in me, but my ways were different. The energy of her youth had been directed and contained to meet conformity, mine was wild, full of self-will. I knew what I wanted but had no notion of where to find it. We had the drink in common and we were family. Moreover, we were Irish and, if nothing else, that would do for a while at least.

I started looking for work. As I had worked in a supermarket at home, I looked there first. Sainsbury's in Lewisham High Street thought I was a worthwhile risk. I know now that they were probably delighted to see a white man come on board, even if he was Irish. My job was trainee manager in the fresh food department. They called it 'fresh food', but it seemed to me that there was nothing fresh in England. Everything was pre-packed, sealed and priced. In Ireland 'fresh' meant cutting it from the carcass, whenever you wanted it.

I was given a uniform and went to the cloakrooms to try it on. I emerged some time later in my chocolate-brown uniform. I lasted a few days. I couldn't take to the toffee-nosed English telling me what to do. However, they owed me money and I had to get it. If I had walked out, my chances of getting it would be slim. I needed a good excuse.

I decided to tell them that word had just arrived from Ireland that my father, a high-ranking soldier in the Irish army, had been killed. He had been operating on a top-secret mission when the tragedy struck, and in order to maintain the mission's cover his death would not be made public. I told them I needed to return to the safety of the army barracks at home, as, being related, my own life was in danger. I remember their faces as I told my story. They didn't know whether to laugh or cry. They gave me my money, and a little extra as well. I thanked them graciously, looked upset and left. I am sure they were glad to see the back of me, and probably got the anti-terrorist squad in just to make sure I hadn't left them any presents.

Once free I went to a pub, called a pint, met a man and told him I was just out of Brixton prison, having served my sentence in the service of my country. Then I got pissed.

Getting pissed in Ireland is one thing, but doing it in England is entirely different. In Ireland a man can say what he likes when he's drunk, because everyone else is saying the same thing. We all start talking about the English and the terrible things they did; we are great republicans when we are drunk.

When I was drunk in a pub in the middle of the High Street in Bromley, down in Kent, I was often heard to lambast my fellow patrons with a multiplicity of verbal abuse relating to the continued occupation of my country by the Queen's forces. It wasn't the place to do it, of course, and I often wondered why I wasn't arrested. I put it down to the absence of a large enough atrocity taking place to haul me in over. While I absolutely detest the British police I have to admit that they are no fools. They probably knew all about me. I thank my lucky stars that I was gone out of England long before any bombs went off, or I could have ended up like the Guildford four or the Birmingham six: an easy arrest and an even easier conviction. An Irishman in England is guilty just because he's Irish. I often wonder how many innocent Irishmen lie rotting in English jails, their only crime shooting their mouths off after consuming too much Strongbow or Kronenberg 1664

I went back to Kent ten years later with my then wife and eldest daughter. We went on a mission to purchase a breed of dog unavailable in Ireland – a Chesapeake Bay retriever. We drove down from London to Rochester and called on the breeder, who had only one puppy left.

The English really look after their animals and I reluctantly have to admit that the Irish I have met could learn a thing or two from them. The family we called on were quite obviously working class and pure salt of the earth. I was introduced to the man of the house, a man called Ron, and my wife spoke to his wife, Betty, while my daughter played with the new pup. It became apparent to me that Ron had a military way about him and my suspicion was confirmed when he told me he worked in security. I talked away none the less, deciding it best not to mention the war. I was really only concerned about getting my dog and getting home in one piece.

The following morning we returned to Betty and Ron's house to pick up our dog, and this time the information flowed a bit more freely. Ron started talking about Ireland, and specifically Northern Ireland.

'What took you over there, Ron?' says I, knowing full well but trying to be as diplomatic as possible. After all, I was standing in his English kitchen.

'I was in the services,' he replied, and I knowing full well that he still was.

'What year were you there?' I asked, trying to look sympathetic, because the North of Ireland is not exactly a trip to the best of holy Catholic Ireland. Indeed, if I was a British soldier – and there is a better chance of hell freezing over as there is of that happening – the North of Ireland is the very last place I'd want to be.

'I was there in '79, '81 and '83,' he replied. I was feeling a familiar hatred rising up in me, because this bastard was clearly a war lord rather than your common I-needed-a-job soldier.

'Jasus, you were there in hard times,' says I looking at the wife, who was by now almost ready to break wind with the stress of it. 'You were there when Bobby died, so,' says I, again turning my attention to the wife, and meaning that bravest of volunteers, Bobby Sands, who died while on hunger strike in the Maze in 1981. He was the first of the hunger strikers to die and the whole world mourned him, for he was a true Irish hero. 'It was '81 that Bob died, wasn't, it love?' I continued, just to make sure that the war lord was left in no doubt that a republican was standing in his English kitchen.

'We had better go,' says the wife, her eyes pleading.

'Okay so, thanks for everything,' says I as we left, and the poor bastard wondering should he call MI5 or not.

That night as I sat on the plane at Heathrow waiting for take-off I started reading *Borstal Boy* by Brendan Behan. I had bought it earlier in the duty-free shop, along with *Confessions of an Irish Rebel*. When I read how poor Brendan was arrested after less than forty-eight hours in Liverpool, I thanked God and all his angels and saints, as the plane left the ground heading for the Emerald Isle, that I was not being detained at Her Majesty's pleasure and some whore of a policeman squeezing the life out of my balls.

The lesson was not lost on me, however, and I now considered my part in the peace process complete. Not that I had ever taken part in the war; well, not really.

*   *   *

The centre of London is a strange place. The city has lots of character, but the people have none. I liked it and spent a lot of time there. I was a great walker and often headed in the direction of Buckingham Palace. I used to stop along the way and have a drink.

I lived most of the time in fantasy land and the drink helped the fantasies to develop. My favourite one, while in the vicinity of the Palace, was to pretend that I was a self-contained 'Active Service Unit', with lumps of semtex hanging out of my arse. Like a Ninja I'd slip unnoticed over the wall and past the guards. The

Queen's quarters would be my target. I'd prime the semtex, set the timer and run like hell! My return to Ireland would be a glorious one. People from all over Ireland would converge on the capital as my canoe docked by O'Connell Bridge with six days of beard on me. I'd be hoisted up by blondes and brunettes and I'd be whisked away by a waiting limo and on to the waiting crowd outside the Guinness brewery. There I'd be given the Freedom of Guinness's and a room opposite with a brothel beneath.

Back in reality I was pissed as a coot in Charing Cross, got the train to Lee and felt the wrath of my waiting aunt.

The Irish are supposed to look after their own. You might stab a Cork man in Dublin, but put the same man alongside yourself anywhere in the world – except Ireland, of course – and you should be preventing any harm coming to the bastard.

While I didn't meet any Irish that actually did me any harm, I didn't meet any that looked out for me either. I found the ones I met to be a sorry shower of bastards. It was sad really. I was certainly left in no doubt as to how we'd got our reputation. The pubs of London were full of washed-up drunks all crying into their beer and lamenting their lost years. The successful Irish, of which there are many, I never met. They didn't go into the pubs like the Irish I met. Therein lies the answer.

Ten weeks after I emigrated, I was deported. My aunt brought me to Heathrow, bought me a ticket, told me she never wanted to see me again and left. I got on the plane, shit a brick and tried to get some sleep.

Spirituality

My mother was at the airport to meet me, but definitely not to greet me. We drove home in silence and, without ceremony, I went to my room. I was stone broke, so there was no point in going anywhere else.

Later I was called for my dinner. My brother, the bastard, was loving it. The meal passed off in silence. It was Wednesday night and a crowd of bible thumpers were due to arrive, a regular Wednesday night event. They'd all pray and speak in tongues and go back to their sick and sad lives around ten o'clock. The old man couldn't lose his head before the prayers, so I was saved until it was over at least.

My father had recovered from his depression some years earlier. The reason for his depression has been the subject of much debate. Whether it was chemical or emotional or both I don't know. I do know that his own family had theories relating to the mother breaking his balls. I can go along with that, knowing what I know now. Whatever the cause, the cure was religion. He was mad into the charismatic renewal movement. Every Wednesday night for a good number of years he held a prayer

meeting. All sorts came. There were faith healers, pretend alcoholics, depressives, mental retards (God love them – they were
harmless), and then there were the spiritualists. The latter were
the most dangerous of all. They were on a major ego trip and I
think they actually believed they had a direct line to God. I didn't
agree with any of it, but who am I to judge? It got the old man
through the night, and whatever gets you through that is fine by
me.

I went for a walk, but I only had twenty-four pence, so I couldn't
even buy a cigar; the cheapest was thirty-one pence. I walked
down by the local pub and back by the shop. I met an old drinking buddy, a fella in his fifties, who said he was surprised to see
me. I told him it hadn't work out in England, that I was broke and
that I'd love a pint. He told me that he'd see me around and headed off for the pub. His wife left him a few years later so I look him
off my hit list.

I went back home around 9.30 hoping to bum a fag off one of
the religious pricks, but no such luck. They were all too spiritual
for that. I wandered aimlessly around the house trying to scratch
my itch, but only one thing could scratch that and, in its absence,
the itch stayed.

I was summoned to the 'State rooms' at 10.30. My loving
mother, my father and I sat facing each other. I felt I was going to
be thrown out and got a bit nervous. Then Dad started talking.
He told me I had a drink problem and that I had to stop. I felt like
telling him that the only problem I had was sitting beside him,
but decided not to because I didn't fancy going back to the
bridge again. He said that the drinking would have to stop or I'd
have to go. This time it would be for good.

There is something about a conclusion that gives a man a bit
of peace. The conclusion might not be the one you want, but at
least you know where you are going. I knew where I stood. I
wasn't happy, but I wasn't sad either. At least I had a bed.

Security

A mad looking bastard with a red car, long curly hair and a pair of cowboy boots met with me one night, a meeting which had been arranged. He had a middle-aged woman with him. She was from the flats and looked like the tolerant type. They brought me to a big hall where everyone was talking about drink. To my disgust they hadn't got any, so I left. Nobody followed me, and that was that. I met the fella with curly hair again a short time later. I grew to like him and trust him. I consider him a close friend now, because he has stood the test of time. He was and is genuine and has always been a great support. I don't think I'd have made it without him. It isn't that he did anything special, he was just there and his door was always open. He never turned me away and he never looked for anything. He was just a friend and I would go to the ends of the earth for him. I also know how to be a friend.

It was killing me not to drink, but I needed a bed. I was under pressure. The most important thing in the world is to know that the roof over your head isn't under threat. If a man has that he can start to do something for himself. Threats and me never worked well together.

A man told me one night, as we slept under the milky way, that a man's health is his wealth. If a man has his health he has everything. I started to think about that, but my deliberations led in a frightening direction, so I stopped.

When I went home in the evenings, having spent my day at work, looking for work, I was constantly reminded of how near to the door I was. But I had a deal, and the old fella and I were sticking to it. They couldn't touch me.

I got a job and the old fella got sick. He was shipped off to hospital and my world was under threat again. The da was very sick and everyone said he was going to die, but the everyone that was always right was once again wrong. He is still around, God bless him.

The mother and the brother spent their time in Dublin holding his hand, hoping he'd die. He had given them nothing but trouble, but they couldn't get rid of him the way they had me. The brother wasn't wasting any time. He was driving the da's car and he went looking for his will. He even went to the bank to find out if he could get his hands on the money, if and when the da croaked it. The da knows all this but says nothing. I think that is his trouble – he doesn't stand up for himself. He is a good man. He is well liked and I like him too. I accept him for what he is and above all I respect him. He has a lot to offer and it has nothing to do with money.

When they were all in Dublin I got my chance. I went on the piss, and an unmerciful piss at that. I was so bad that I was even walking around with the fly of my pants open. The guy I was working for was as bad: a martyr for porter. We drank our loafs off seven days a week and even when my mother came home I didn't give a shit. I thought they'd never throw me out with the old fella dying. I was wrong.

I went to work one morning, seedy as usual, and commenced my day in the best possible manner. Around midday I decided to go to the labour exchange to sign on. I hadn't told them that I was working. The office I worked in was up a narrow flight of stairs, and a small hallway led to the street. I went out through the hall and noticed some familiar looking bags and walked on. Halfway to the labour exchange I froze. I started to tremble and realised the worst. I ran back to the hallway and my bags greeted me. I was homeless again.

When a woman has sex, she knows the risks. If she's caught there's no way out, at least there wasn't in the 1960s. If there's no way out she gets on with it. She could, of course, put the baby up for adoption and be done with it, but that's hard, and, if she's married, unheard of. From the moment my mother brought me home she was trying to get rid of me. From my earliest memories, she was sending me away. I was never sure what was going to happen next. I'm sure she had her problems, but an adult's problems should never become a child's. Childhood is precious, and should be nurtured. Mine wasn't. When I reached ten, she would often be heard to say 'I wish you were old enough to go away, get your own place, and leave us in peace.' My brother was her lapdog and I was never secure. My mother ran from her responsibilities; she ran from me. I was her responsibility. I have children now and I'll never run, no matter how bad it gets. Anyway, I love them and love doesn't run.

I couldn't go back to the streets. Those days were gone. I went to my boss, told him the story, and he got suddenly busy. I knew where I stood. I placed him on the hit list, another man for Libyan horse feed.

I walked the streets – frighteningly familiar – and the rage grew. I sought out familiar haunts, saw familiar faces and silently I screamed. Paranoia set in. People were looking, they knew. Some were laughing, others sneering, some looked away and others stared. They all knew. My mother had told them. I went to a priest, but he couldn't help. I walked for hours, my mind racing, my nerves jumping. I thought of the river, and a mid-winter swim. I hadn't the courage, so I walked on. I decided to phone, to plead my case: it was −2°C and I had no coat. The phone was answered and I said 'hello' and heard a click.

In desperate times, people do desperate things. I had heard of a man that threw a barrel through a window and waited for the cops to come. They came, and he got a bed. But that was too temporary; something more permanent was needed.

I went to a café where fellas that used to drink, and don't anymore, tend to go. I went in and saw a fellow who was off the drink for years. He knew the score. I told him I had a compulsion, stronger than ever, to go and get drunk. I pleaded for help. He suggested that I go to hospital and I asked him to take me. Up the street and onto another we went, and in through the gates of the madhouse.

Treatment

Ireland was full of hard men, hard women and bitter children. When the children got older the bitterness turned to hardness and the cycle continued. Weakness was shunned. It wasn't allowed, it had to be hidden. You didn't have to be mad to go into a madhouse, just weak. When you were in, you became mad anyway, and everyone relaxed because they knew they were right all along. But privately they knew they were wrong.

The weak and the restless, the mentally handicapped, even the physically handicapped, made up the population of Ireland's mental institutions. Everything that was less than perfect was locked away, forgotten and disinherited.

My local mental hospital was full of such people. Old men, deformed at birth, were thrown in there because one leg was shorter than the other, or one hand was facing the wrong way round. The real truth was that the evil men that had fathered them wouldn't feed them, because their work would be unproductive. Women had no say, they were baby factories procreating for the Church in loveless marriages. It suited the Church for human imperfection to be hidden, where it didn't have to be explained – whereas, in truth, nothing that God creates needs to be.

I met a man during my stay in the madhouse who had spent forty-six years taking their drugs, being told he was mad, his freedom removed and no hope of escape. His only crime was that, when drunk, he had exposed himself to a girl whose father was wealthy. He was only sixteen and was locked up for life. His local community had arranged it all – the priest, the guard, the head teacher, his parents and the doctor. When I met him he wasn't mad, just institutionalised and addicted to the drugs.

I was put in assessment, where they decided what they'd do with you, where you'd go and how long you'd be kept. The place smelt of piss and fags. Everyone smoked, all day every day; there was nothing else to do. The conditions being treated were varied: depression, drugs, booze and nervous breakdowns. The treatment was the same. Fuck all! They took people into hospital and fed them with drugs so that, when they left, instead of having one problem they had two. The patients were never spoken to, never listened to – and I am sure that some of them just needed to talk. Their backgrounds were all the same, poor and helpless, or destitute and fucked. I was the latter.

There were a few who were in for the booze and I teamed up with them. Once the booze is gone and the back is to the wall, the booze lover can be a cunning bastard. The lads I met knew the score. They knew what they wanted and what they needed more than the doctors or nurses did. We all had one thing in common – survival. An 'alky' is a born survivor – if he wasn't, there would be no alkys.

I was just there for the bed. After a while I suppose I was prepared to talk about the drink, but at the end of the day I believed I knew what was best and no one else did. The professionals only saw one side of things, but I saw them all.

In those days the system moved slowly. There was no structure and no one really knew what to do. A nun (the Church again!) was running a treatment facility near the mental hospital, but it only operated during the day. She was supposed to have a massive success rate. Anyone that went through her programme came off the sauce – and that was what mattered.

A fella I used to call 'Flat Nose Davy' was one of the nun's 'success stories'. He was a hard case and had been on the bottle for years. His style of drinking was the park bench. Self-delusion had left him years earlier, he just wanted to get buckled, and the cheapest most direct way to do it was by the bottle. The ambience of the pub meant nothing to Davy, and conversation meant even less. He was the hardest case I've ever known, but I liked him a lot.

For a short time Davy was 'cured'. He got cleaned up, had a haircut and shaved his beard. The shakes were under control and his voice was audible. With every passing day Davy got better and the nun was delighted. The last time I saw Davy I wished him the comfort of a quick death. Those words of humility came to mind: 'but for the grace of God, there go I'. I felt for Davy and I thanked God for saving me. I have always believed that I am only as good as my last sale. It's a pity someone didn't tell this to the nun and maybe the poor souls she told were cured might have been in with a chance.

A nurse in the hospital, a good fellow, sent me to see the nun. She was like a lot of nuns I'd known – a proper bitch. I was trapped, like an animal but worse – you'd respect an animal. She introduced me to her 'success stories' and closed the door; I wasn't good enough to be one of them. Then she gave me a test. There was 550 questions, all very repetitive. I must have completely confused them and often wondered what the results were. The way she ran from me the next time I met her, I think I must have come out as a serial rapist.

The nurse that had sent me to the nun decided to try and get me out of the madhouse and into somewhere more stable. He succeeded. I met him years later, when I got on a boat somewhere off the west coast of Ireland. The boat had other people on it and no one knew my history. He winked at me and smiled. I smiled back. I had a good day's fishing.

Charity

In among all the bad people I have met – and they were many –someone good always happened to come along at the right time. I'm only talking about ten at the most in an entire lifetime – as a percentage of all the people I have met it's very small – but they were very important. That nurse was one. Thanks, Tommy. (Another was a politician, 'Big Jim'. The man is dead now and a great loss.)

After leaving the madhouse, I got a flat and went back on the dole. The health board gave me a tenner towards the rent. It was dire poverty, but, let's face it, I wasn't the only one and at least I was off the streets. I had thirty-five pounds to live on for an entire week. I got the money on a Tuesday and, if I went on the piss, I starved for a week. I did that a couple of times and stayed in bed to kill the rest of the week – a trick learned from earlier experience. I remembered the hunger strikes in '81 and all the great men that died, Bobby Sands the first. No one cared when, like him, I was starving. God rest him and say a prayer.

I bought shoes and forgot I had bought them. It wasn't that they were comfortable, I just got careless. I went on the piss. The money was gone. No money, no rent; no rent, no home; no home, the streets – no way. I had a fiver left, but I needed twenty. My back was to the wall (it had never really left it).

I had fallen in with a new crowd, and none of them drank. I decided I'd tell them. I did, and guess what? I couldn't go back to the St. Vincent de Paul – they were still at No. 1 on the hit list. I went to the priests and got no joy, everyone turned their backs. The streets were looming and I began to panic. I couldn't go back and only one option remained: the river. I walked the streets, my stomach in a knot. The desperation was terrible. Then a thought came: the politicians might help. Maybe they could get me an advance from the health board and I'd be safe for a while at least. I went to see Big Jim.

I told him my story and he listened in silence. I expected him to make a call, to divert my enquiry, to pass the buck. He didn't. He gave me the twenty pounds and saved my life. I promised him my vote for ever more and left; and I always gave it. Before he died I saw him on the street, stopped my car and, in a shining new suit, approached him. I asked him if he remembered me and he did. I offered him back the twenty, but he wouldn't take it. He wished me well, told me to keep it up and that he was proud of me. When I learned of his death I said a silent prayer. His body went to the grave without the Church, for he didn't believe. I have no doubt that he is now sitting in the shadow of God, for he saved one life and probably more.

I stayed off the drink and looked for a job. Day in and day out, with a burning desire and desperate urgency, I searched. I set targets and discovered some truths. Security meant work. Work meant money, money meant independence and independence meant safety. I needed to be safe. Looking for work is a thankless task, unless you get the job. I knocked at doors, banged at doors, roared at doors, but no work came.

FÁS, the State employment agency, specialised in taking people off the live register and placing them on training programmes for jobs that didn't exist. It looked good for the government, because the unemployment figures went down. If employers wanted somebody to work cheaply and for a short time, they went to FÁS. Occasionally there was a good job, and if you were lucky you got it. I got it but I wasn't lucky. I pissed an official off so badly that he got me the job just to get rid of me.

I was sent to a hotel one morning for a job interview with a man called John. I had to stick the sole of my shoe on because it had started to lift. There was a hole in the knee of my right trouser leg as well, so I kept my legs crossed so he wouldn't see it.

'Yeah, sure, how are ya doin'?' says he, and I recognised his type straight away. He was the type that liked power and loved to feel big. He was a small man with a wrinkled bitter face and deceitful eyes. I did a good interview and I told him what he wanted to hear. It was all about feeding his ego. I didn't care, I just wanted a job.

At any rate I got the job and things got better; not easier, just better. I was to start straight away and that wasn't soon enough.

PART TWO

The Twilight Zone

Destinations

I met a group of fellows once who were talking about taking life one day at a time. They seemed to think this was a mind-boggling concept, one which would take a lot of effort to master. I was surprised. I had been taking life a day at a time for twenty years. For me it was a means of survival.

Tradition is very important; without it a society is shallow and meaningless. Traditions change from generation to generation, but they should never go away. The family is still our greatest tra-dition, and all our families form our community.

My mother's people are a strong family, and it is from them that I inherited my sense of family. It certainly wasn't from my mother or any of my immediate family – if I was to be guided by them I would never have had children of my own and would probably have campaigned against having them. Being in a family gives a sense of belonging. This spreads into the community and then into the county and finally to one's country. I never belonged to my family, and as a direct result I never fitted in to my community. I was always homeless even when I had a home.

A secure job with a pension was one tradition. The guards, the post office, multinationals with branded goods, all made for good jobs and good employers. Your life night be boring, worthless and utterly miserable, but once you had a job, a permanent job, you were somebody. It was important to be somebody. The more secure the job, the more you were respected. I decided I needed respect.

Big companies can take a body over. My identity changed the day I went to work for my first multinational. They thought they owned me. They provided the security, the pension, and in my case the car as well. The more you get the more you are expected to give. However, some multinationals are worse than others. The first crowd I worked for were a prime shower of bastards. They trampled on everyone. The crowd I work for now have been good to me. They're human, and understand the meaning of the word humanity. They see people as their greatest asset and, as a result, the people that work for them are their greatest asset.

Abuse is a strange thing. When I thought I was free of the abuser, I still went back. It was as if I needed my family to approve and therefore stop the abuse. It didn't work, of course. I thought my job with the multinational was what they wanted. It marked conformity, my coming of age. Outside opinion and image were important to my family, so when I began to fit the image I went back. They screwed me again. Every time they got an opportunity they interfered. I always – well nearly always – went on the drink afterwards, only to stop again full of guilt. Yet, still I went back for more.

Trust

I don't want to be unkind, so I'll just say my mother had some very strange ways. Everything was going fine in my new job. My father had readmitted me to the family home, and I was getting a break at last. Then John, my boss, decided to phone me at home.

When someone is vulnerable, they trust easily – a bad mistake. Of course, the last people you expect to screw you are your own, but then I'm not a normal man and they're not normal people. I was working in the deep south and, as was part and parcel of life as a commercial traveller, I had to stay away on certain nights. One Tuesday I had to stay in Tralee, in County Kerry, and a fine place it is too. John didn't know where exactly I was and decided he would ring my home at 7.30 p.m. He dialled all night but only got an engaged tone. Little did poor John know that the mother had the phone off the hook. At any rate I wasn't there, and the old lady didn't know where I was even if he had got through.

John got very annoyed. He had lost his night's sleep. He was a bit of a control freak and being unable to contact anyone who was in his charge would nearly have made him suicidal. I, in the meantime, was the guest of that fine Tralee hotel, The Grand, sleeping peacefully and dreaming my own horrors. The following day, I rose at dawn, in accordance with procedure as laid down in the company manual, and commenced my day's work at 9 a.m. as usual.

I had a busy day selling sweets and candy to the grocery trade of Kerry and, having contributed nobly to the betterment of the sweet factory, I hit for home some time in the evening. Upon returning home, I changed my clothes, met no one and went off out for the evening. I returned to the ranch – as I called our three-bedroomed house, notably because of its liking for whips – at about 11pm. I was greeted at the door by my loving mother.

Her eyes were bulging, her lips tight, giving way to the wrinkles on either cheek. I got lambasted.

'You're a bastard,' she told me. 'You bring nothing but trouble to this door.'

I looked at her in disbelief. As far as I was aware I had done nothing wrong. I racked my brain for any loose ends from the past which might be coming back to haunt me. I couldn't think of anything, but, then again, when a fella was drunk as often as I was you can't be too sure.

'What did I do now, you mad cunt?' I shouted at her, deciding that attack was the best form of defence.

'Did you hear that, did you?' she called to my old fella, manipulating him into taking her side – the damsel in distress and knight to the rescue type of shite. 'He called me a cunt, in my own house that I've slaved to put around me,' she wailed.

The old fella appeared, pipe in mouth, sighing in subjection. 'Don't talk to your mother like that, Peter,' he said weakly, hoping for a quick dismissal.

'Ah bollocks!' I said, 'I'm only in the door and she started. I did fuck-all, but she has to be bitching about something,' I shouted as I brushed past him heading for the kitchen.

'John rang here tonight and abused me because he was

80

ringing you all night last night and couldn't get you,' the mother shouted after me. 'It's my phone and if I want to take it off the hook, off the fucking hook I'll take it,' she roared.

A vice grip took hold of my testicles. The boss had been speaking to her! That meant only one thing. Whatever he had rung about, regardless of whether he was in the wrong or not, the mother would have done her best to ruin me. The feeling of being fucked came over me. Whenever I've had that feeling I've never been wrong. It's like the fellow that was on death row for ten years. Every morning for ten years his door opened and everything was fine. The morning he was to be executed the door opened and he shit his pants. I was shitting my pants.

'John said, if he couldn't contact you, you were no good to him. I told him you were no good to him anyway. You might say that I did you, you little bastard!' she shouted at my frozen frame.

She had done it again. I was dumbfounded. The old man was oblivious to everything, the mother was intent on my destruction.

'What in the name of God did you say to him?' I cried. 'I only work for him, he doesn't own me. I'm twenty-one years old. Jesus! Jesus! Why can't you mind your own business?' I screamed.

'You *are* my business. I have to warn people, so they won't be blaming me when they discover what you're like. I did my best, and they'll know I did my best. Don't have anyone else ringing this house, do your hear? That's my phone, mine, and mine alone. The sooner we're rid of you the better.'

The outburst complete, she made for the stairs. I looked at my old fella. If he gave a toss, he didn't say so.

'Go to bed,' he said. 'It'll be all right.' How could it be all right? It was never all right. I needed a drink.

Interrogation

I was desperately insecure and felt very inferior. I think my whole family felt the same, but they dealt with it better than I did, or in different ways.

The world is full of bastards, they spot the weak and, like vultures, they prey. The worst type are those whose motives are purely sadistic. Some of these are drinkers. The fact that they abuse drink doesn't make them nice little huggy bears who destroy themselves and those they love while blindly trying to save themselves. Even if they stopped drinking it wouldn't change the very basis of their personality, it just makes it harder to spot. A sober bastard is a cunning bastard. I was never a bastard. I only acted like one when one was near. It was a defence mechanism, but unfortunately it wasn't finely tuned. I'm too soft really and just wanted to be loved.

My mother had revealed the lot. She had hung me out to dry and made a total fool of me. It wasn't the first time nor the last. Her best was yet to come.

John got in touch with me the day after my mother's outburst. He was very serious and had his 'I am the boss' voice well oiled. My defences went up, and twenty years of survival came into play.

'I'd like to see you on Friday,' he instructed.

'Of course, John,' I said. 'Any time in particular?'

'Three o'clock, in the car park of Crazy Prices,' he replied, and he hung up.

This was serious. He wasn't meeting me in a public place where passers-by could hear. He was meeting me in his car, that triumph of Japanese engineering in which he could feel bigger than he truly was.

I couldn't work. I couldn't sleep. The fear grew and grew in intensity. Eventually I couldn't even eat, an unusual one for me. I never usually missed a meal, whether I was hungry or not, because you learn when you've slept rough that you never know when you're going to eat next. Once a man has slept rough he always sleeps rough; even if he is in the Ritz with caviare and blondes, in his head he is on the street.

Diarrhoea came as the fear grew, then the headache as panic set in. Paranoia took over, and I imagined the worst. Twenty-four hours can be an eternity. I wrote a speech, pre-empting what John might say. He wasn't going to have the last word.

Three o'clock Friday arrived amidst a herald of diarrhoea and puke and a feeling of impending doom.

'Yeah sure, how are you?' asked John, pretending to be my buddy, my confidante and general all-round nice guy. He didn't fool me. I was ready for the bastard.

'I'm great, John,' I replied, 'and your good self?'

'Yeah sure, I'm fine, just fine,' he said as he fumbled with his black leather folder, which shone with newness and importance. 'Tell me,' says he, 'I think I've been a fair man up to now. I'd like to think I'm approachable and I try to be understanding.' I began to sweat, wondering where this line of bullshit was leading. 'If you had anything to tell me, I'd like to think you'd be able to speak to me, as a friend,' he said.

Jesus! I thought, where is this going? Wherever it was going it was going in the wrong direction. I had imagined it differently. He sat there, the sun beating in the window on his striped shirt, waiting for my reply. I wondered if he was genuine or not. Was he being fatherly, helpful and all that goes with it, or was he just setting me up. I didn't know. Anyone who had been fatherly in the past had hurt me. I wondered should I take a chance.

'What exactly are you talking about?' I asked.

'I'll leave that up to you,' he replied.

This was all new. I was under pressure, my back was to the wall. I knew what he wanted to hear, but didn't know why he wanted to hear it. What was his motive? Was he going to give me a two-week holiday in Spain because I had had a tough time, or was he going to fire me? Worse still, was he going to keep me on and use it against me whenever it suited him?

I was a rat stuck in a corner, my choices narrowed: tell him to fuck off, or lay myself at his mercy. I chose the latter.

'This has to do with what the old lady told you, I presume?' I said, making a prostitute of myself but still trying to keep some dignity.

'Yeah sure, you know yourself,' he replied, watching me squirm. I let it all out.

'The drink, John, it's about the drink. I had to give it up because I couldn't handle it, it's as simple as that. I don't drink now and I'm working at staying off it, and I'm doing okay.' It was over, my privacy was gone and I had just told someone about myself who didn't need to know a thing. Thanks, Mammy!

'Yeah sure, I'm delighted you told me. It's better when someone makes a clean breast of things. Good man,' he said as he opened his folder, pretending he was doing something and that what I had just said didn't really matter.

'So what now ?' I asked. 'Does this make a difference to me keeping my job?' I asked in fear, my voice starting to tremble.

'Yeah sure, we'll see. So long now and I'll be in touch,' he said, dismissing me.

I'll give you 'yeah sure', you bastard, I thought, with your poxy little body and wrinkled old face.

'Good luck so, John,' I said, opening the door of the car. 'Have a nice weekend.'

'Yeah sure, all the best,' he replied, never raising his eyes from his freebie company folder. I took one long look at him and put him on the hit list.

I walked away, my world falling apart, the streets looming. No job, no money; no money, no home. The tension was killing. I walked to my car and got in. Jesus, I thought, where does it all end? I'm only packing shelves with sweets, I'm not a staff member in the Pentagon. I vowed to get him, to get them all.

I went home and packed a bag. I was going on the piss. I couldn't drink and go home, so I headed for Newry for the weekend, 200 miles away, where no one would know me and no one would know what I had done.

The Hang Men

I drank for the weekend and then stopped, the guilt back and my confidence gone. I began to hate and struggled for air. John didn't mention our little chat again, there was just a difference in his eyes when he looked at me. It was a look that said 'no matter what you do, it'll never make a difference'. However, he sent me letters of warning for every conceivable misdemeanour.

I remember one time I was sent on relief selling in the southeast. The guy that was supposed to be doing it was off sick. He gave me the stock cards and told me to give them back to him at the forthcoming sales meeting. I did as I was told and kept the cards. Then John rang.

I have always had a sense of loyalty. Honour among thieves and all that sort of thing. You never hang another guy, you never snitch to the cops. My brother taught me that. He was a hanging bastard, always snitching to the mother or father. John wanted to know why I hadn't posted the cards back, so I told him and he hung up. Then he rang back. The other guy said I was lying, that he had told me to post back the cards. Call me a fool, call me anything you like, but I didn't fight. I think I was right. One way or another I was going to be in the wrong, and if it wasn't this time it would be another. John would see to that.

Amazingly, it emerged later that the guy that did the dirty on me was demoted and sent back to Dublin, where he was from. He had a serious gambling problem and was constantly in the bookie's. He didn't lose his job, because his daddy was a former managing director of the company. I feel for this chap and his problem – gambling is a terrible thing and I detest it with a passion – but I'll never forgive him for discrediting me.

At any rate, I got a letter telling me that, should I get another letter, that was it, curtains. The hounds were close. I got a familiar feeling – I needed to escape.

I had finally managed to get my act together. I wasn't drinking, except for the odd time – in remote locations, although not as far as Newry – and I felt like shite each time, bad enough to keep me off it until the next time, and eventually there was no next time, at least for a good few years.

The people I dealt with were mainly OK, but there were a few bastards as well. I had such low self-esteem that I automatically assumed that everyone I met was better. And if they were nice to me I weakened – the defences went down.

Two fellas went on my hit list about this time. One was a trainee manager and the other a security guard with whom I had drunk on many an occasion in the past. I haven't seen the trainee manger in years, but the security guard is still at it, drinking his loaf off and going from dead end job to dead end job.

I built an Easter egg display in a supermarket one night, trying to keep John happy. I stayed there late and finished the job. The next day, I went to do a different display and was greeted by my devious trainee manager.

'You'll have to do that display again,' said he, pointing to the Easter egg display that I had lovingly erected the night before.

'Ah, Jesus,' I said, 'you can't be fucking serious!'

Just then the aforementioned imitation policeman happened to pass. You'd swear it was planned.

'Did you hear that?' shouted the trainee to the security man.

'I did, I did indeed,' he replied, not having a clue what the trainee was talking about. I saw the trainee wink.

'That's it,' said he, 'you won't tell me to fuck off again. I'll have you barred from this shop.'

'I didn't tell you to fuck off,' I retorted, looking at the security guard for mercy. But if Judas denied Christ, this bastard would deny his own child.

'I heard you,' said the guard, and they both headed off in the direction of the manager's office to lodge their complaint, leaving me to stew beside a perfect end display.

Supermarket managers had great power over people in my line of work. They were generally oppressed by their superiors, working crazy hours and generally becoming bitter bastards. But they controlled shelf space, and shelf space was selling space. If I couldn't get on with a manager, or couldn't get space, I was no good. Surplus to requirements. To be barred from a store was a death sentence.

The manager arrived on the scene, cordless phone to his ear, having a conversation with my big boss – bigger than John, and that's big! He was telling him that I was barred from the shop and no reprieve would be given. No one was going to tell his trainee to fuck off.

I left the shop in a panic. I had only one option, and that was to go to a colleague of the manager – his equal in a bigger store – and ask him to intercede on my behalf. When I draw up my list of the top ten people, this guy will be one of them. I met Dave and told him my tale of woe. He saw the seriousness of the situation and offered to help. He rang the manager in the other store and told him to call off the dogs. Then he rang my boss, the big boss, and apologised on behalf of his colleague. The big boss didn't know what hit him, having a supermarket manager apologise to him! I was a hero. That was a long time ago and all the managers have changed, several times over, but Dave remains and is liked by all.

The way people interfere in a man's life never fails to amaze me. I remember one Sunday afternoon, coming back from an FCA weekend (the Reserve Army), I passed out one of the officers – and a captain at that. He was only an FCA captain, however, and as such didn't command the same respect as a regular army man, captain or not. The following week I met John and he dragged me over the coals because the pretend soldier had squealed. I find it impossible to understand what motivated him. What was in it for him?

The FCA were a great bunch in general. I joined up with them after I had left the Dominicans. It was a great pastime and many a great piss-up I had with them. The most wonderful thing about it was that a volunteer could turn up whenever he liked. They couldn't control you. I used to stay away for months at a time, generally when things were bad. When I'd arrive back they would make a fuss of me, hoping I'd stay and keep their numbers up in order to qualify for funding.

I used to enjoy the shooting and the pomp and ceremony associated with marching on St. Patrick's day and similar occasions. I think, as well, that being part of an army, and an Irish army at that, gave me a sense of pride, and more importantly a sense of belonging.

It was this feeling of belonging that made me stop at Barna Gap one bright and sunny morning. Barna Gap on the Limerick and Kerry border is famous for one of the biggest raids in the history of the Irish State which took place there in 1979. The IRA was said to have been responsible. The significance of the location was lost on me, however, as I pulled in beside a number of Irish army Land Rovers. My army kit lay all over the back of my car and signalled to my comrades-at-arms that I was one of them, albeit a part-timer, or as they put it a Fool Carrying Arms, making irreverent reference to the name of my proud force of men.

They left in a hurry and I followed at a safe distance travelling towards Kerry. I was fantasising about carrying out daring raids under the cover of darkness in occupied territory and being a true Irish hero. I had to leave my comrades behind in Abbeyfeale and continued my lonely journey without them. It being the middle of summer, I had the window rolled down. I got as far as Castleisland and, before I knew what was happening, a gun was in my face and I was on the street, legs apart and a fella in a brown suit asking me where the other three were, along with all the guns.

My comrades had set me up. They were so bored that they had told a pack of lies, frightening the shite out of me. I told the detectives who I was and they checked it out. They rang the job and John heard all about it. He wasn't impressed. He said I had brought the company into disrepute and he sent me a letter of warning. There I was serving my country and I was still getting the shit.

Love

Things weren't great, but at the same time they weren't bad. Then I met a woman. In fairness, it wasn't my fault. If my family had minded their own business, I would never have ended up in that mess.

I had proved to them that I could stop drinking. I had stopped for months upon months, but still they weren't happy. My job was wrong; it was traditional but it was still wrong. I shouldn't be smoking, because I had asthma. They even accused me of seeing a married woman – which I was, but it was none of their business! But I didn't give in, I didn't drink. I proved to everyone that I could do it. They kept at me and at me, and eventually I could take no more. I had to get away, I needed to be on my own, so I took off for a few days' camping.

The first two hours were great. There I was out in the wilds, nobody but me, a fishing rod, a can of worms, a lake full of trout and all the space I needed. It was heaven. Then it began to get dark. As dusk enveloped me, so did the midges. They surrounded my head, they got in my hair, in my ears, up my nose, they even got into my eyes! I couldn't take any more. I had to get out of there. I threw my tent, my rod and all my other gear into the back of my car. Heaven had turned into hell – the story of my life.

I started driving, but I didn't know where to go. It was too late to camp somewhere else, and I couldn't book into a hotel at eleven o'clock at night. I drove towards home; there was nowhere else to go. I drove too fast. I told myself to slow down, there was no hurry. How could I go home while they were all still awake? The brother would have me for supper. 'Look, Mam, the great white hunter is home, ha, ha, ha. Ah, baba John-John, were you afraid of the bogey-man?' No, there was no way I was going home to let the bastard gloat over me.

I decided I'd wait until they were all asleep, then I'd sneak in. I'd get up in the morning and head off again. If the brother opened his mouth, I'd castrate him on the spot. I drove through the last village. Only five more miles and I was back in the city. I looked at my watch and it was still only half past twelve. I couldn't go home until at least three.

I drove around the city centre, up the main street, left onto a side street. There were bouncers on the doors of all the night-clubs. I looked at my watch again – it was quarter to one. There was no point in going drinking, the bars in the discos would be closed in an hour. I didn't want a drink anyway, I was afraid of it.

I decided to go into Nitelight's. I'd have a couple of Ballygowans and I'd pass the hour. I told myself that I might even meet my married woman and within the hour my member at least could be going home, whatever about me. I paid the five pounds to the woman at the cash desk. She handed me my ticket and I touched the tips of her fingers. She was warm. I smelt her. Christ, it was nice. I stripped her naked and fondled her breasts.

Some asshole appeared and slipped his hand around her neck and let it dangle freely in front of her protruding nipple. I looked at her. I looked at him. I turned away and walked down the stairs and I cursed them. They thought they had it made, but

I was going places, and one day when I walk in there it wouldn't be a fiver they'd be asking me for, it would be my autograph.

The place was jammed. I looked down at all the heads from my elevated position on the stairs. I told myself that each head represented a fiver. I saw the owner in the corner, surrounded by attentive young dollies, and calculated how much he was making. I hated him. I looked at all the heads again. They were like sardines squashed into a John West tin. I decided to sqeeze in anyway. I told myself that first thing in the morning I would ring the chief fire officer. I would demand that he closed the place down. I'd give that bastard John West.

I pressed my way in towards the top bar. There was a waster at the bar nursing a pint of lager and I asked him if he wanted me to drink it for him. He told me to go and fuck myself. He called me a no-good lush. I wondered if I should hit him but decided not to. I remembered that the bouncers didn't like me. The fools would have taken his side.

I called for a Ballygowan. The barman asked me if I would like it in a glass or in a bottle of gin. The waster beside me thought it was hilarious. I told the barman to give me my drink and to watch his mouth. I got my drink and I handed him a tenner.

The barman came back with my change. He asked me how long I was on the dry. I told him that I was off it eight months, and that maybe he should try it. He said that he didn't have to – he hadn't got the Virus. I wanted to shove my glass of water into his chicken-poxed face. He told me to keep it up, that it suited me. I couldn't hit him then.

I turned away from the bar and looked at the waster. He still hadn't drunk any more of his beer. Good drink is wasted on people like him. I looked at the smug grin on his face and I told him that if he didn't take the stupid grin off his face I'd cut off his balls and shove them down his throat. He lost the grin.

I made my way back to the end of the stairs. I stood against the wall in front of the women's toilet, took out a fag and lit it. The owner and his dollies were gone. He was probably upstairs in his private office, having his member serviced, the lucky bastard.

The girls were coming in and out of the toilet. My married woman hadn't appeared. Maybe she wasn't there. I felt sad for my member.

There was a drunk woman looking into my face. Where had she sprung from? I hadn't seen her going into the toilet. She was telling me that I was gorgeous, that I had beautiful brown eyes. I felt like telling her to piss off, but I was afraid she would throw her drink at me. At any rate, my member told me to keep my mouth shut. I asked her what her name was, but someone pulled her away. That was it, I couldn't take any more. I had to get out of there. I finished my Ballygowan and walked back up the stairs. The dolly was gone with all her fivers. She'd probably taken them up to wipe the owner.

I walked down the main street and headed for the chipper. I got my chips and walked to my car. There were taxis across the road, waiting for people to come out of the discos so that they could take them home and rob them into the bargain. The girl that had told me I was gorgeous was falling across the road. If she hadn't been so drunk she would have been nice. She got in beside one of the robbers across the road.

The taxi was pulling away and I wondered if I should follow. I told myself that I should, that the taxi driver might try more than just robbing her. The taxi went out the west road and I followed at a safe distance. They pulled into a twenty-four hour shop and the girl got out.

I followed her into the shop, where she was buying twenty cigarettes. I decided to say hello. After all, if I made a fool of myself she wouldn't remember in the morning. She turned and faced me. Jesus! she remembered me. She wasn't that drunk after all. I began to panic. I was making a fool of myself. It's at times like that a man needs a drink. She asked me to drive her home, as she didn't like the taxi driver, and I agreed.

She paid the driver and he winked at me. My member told me

94

that he was happy. I told him that I was happy. The girl got into my car and I asked her for directions. She gave me her address and we left.

She was annoying me with stupid drink talk, but I didn't care. We got to her house and she told me her name. She said I couldn't come in, because her mother was in bed. My member was fit to strangle me. I asked her if she would like to go to the coast the following day and she said she'd love to. Then she kissed me.

I stopped my car outside my home. It was quarter to three. They were surely asleep. I went in and made for the stairs in the darkness. I went up trying to be as quiet as possible. Shit! My mother had her light on.

She asked me what I was doing home and I told her I had met a girl. I told her the girl's name. My wonderful mother told me to stay away from the girl. When I asked her why, she wouldn't tell me. I made my mind up not to stay away. The girl sounded interesting.

Crash

Speed is a killer, but, when you're twenty-one, pissed off and in a rage and happen to find yourself behind the wheel of a car, you don't think too much about it.

The morning I smashed the car, the company car at that (whoops John), was no different to any other, except that it was Sunday and Sunday mornings are boring. I woke early, but at ten o'clock on a Sunday morning anyone half normal is fast asleep, or having a wank, or trying to get herself to do it for him. I decided to go for a drive.

I was still in the early days of my relationship with my current wife and I decided to drive by her house to see if anything was stirring; nothing was. The road she lived on is an old road. It's winding and bumpy and full of blind bends – like the new ones, but narrower. It runs adjacent to the main road, which itself once was, and is, a regular route for the drunken driver. I know it well.

I drove off at a fairly nifty speed. My car was a typical company issue, a 1200cc station wagon. The passenger seat was destroyed with gallop stains. The bastard that had it before me must have been riding like a pig. On I went, lowering the foot, preparing for take-off. I went into one particularly bad pot-hole and whacked my head off the side window. I decided to go faster and whack the bastard of a car back. A humpback bridge, previously unnoticed, appeared from nowhere. I left the road, sailing high, ears popping.

Back on earth, I struggled to regain my composure as I faced into the worst bastard of a blind bend. As I went round it two men driving a jeep came out of nowhere. Instinct took over. I looked at the ditch, then at the jeep, I measured my distance and took aim. Four-eyes the driver dropped his jaw, stuck out his tongue and an uglier sight I have never seen. His passenger took cover, sticking his head into the glove compartment. I passed at warp speed, with inches to spare . . . and then I saw the trailer.

It wasn't fair. Again I measured, took aim, but forgot the wheels. All I can remember is the bang. I sat in silence hearing the odd crack and clang of metal as it met with the road, and thought of John. Oh Jesus, John!

Four-eyes came to the window (or what had been the window), followed by his friend.

'Are you all right?' he asked, telling me how stupid he was.

'I'm fine,' I said. 'How the fuck do you think I am?'

'Call an ambulance,' said four-eyes, turning to his friend, suddenly remembering how to use his brain.

'Sure, sure, oh right, oh right, right, right you are. I will, I will indeed, okay so,' replied his dyslexic friend.

I wondered if I had any pain and decided i had. I had cleared the jeep, but the trailer was surely an unsafe load or something like that. I had pains all right, fifty grand's worth.

'I need a doctor,' I moaned, my condition worsening by the second.

'It's on its way,' said four-eyes. 'It'll be here any minute.'

I began to wonder if he had called the air corps. Then I saw the guards arriving. The rotten bastard!

Ordinarily I have time for the guards. They're certainly not the worst bunch I've come across. The French police are ten times worse. I have quite a few guard friends, though I have had run-ins with their colleagues. I have to say, however, that there are bad in every job, and the guards are no different. However, the good ones are very good.

I met a good one once and he was very decent and gave me a break. He could have thrown the book at me. The last time I saw him was in Gort in Co. Galway, while I was stuck in traffic. He was driving an unmarked squad car and he smiled at me. I looked a million dollars and I think he felt he'd made the right decision.

A staunch republican, member of Sinn Féin and, I suspect, former IRA man once said to me that he too thought that most guards do a good job, and that but for them nobody would be able to walk the streets at night. He said he only disagreed with them on one issue. That didn't seem to matter though. Shoot me today, love me tomorrow – fair play to him.

A guard came to the window that was and looked in at me. I knew he was a bad one.

'Are you hurt?' he asked, pretending to care.

'I don't know,' says I, 'I'm not a doctor.' The guard smiled in a fuck-you type of way and started measuring skid marks.

The ambulance came and I decided that it would be best to go with them. To say I wasn't hurt now would only make matters worse. I'd just have to live with the lie.

Into Labour

When John heard the news his waters broke and he went into labour. I sensed a letter. He decided we'd have a case conference and we went to look at the car. The road was, in the cold light of day, very narrow indeed. I knew I was fucked. The chassis of my car had furrowed a channel deep enough to set spuds in. John wasn't the only one giving birth.

The car was a shambles. The front right wing didn't exist and the door was buckled, and instead of feeling lucky I felt sick.

'Yeah sure, you're a fine pilot,' says John, his mouth tightening. 'Bill will be fairly pissed off when he sees this. Yeah sure, you should get a job in the RAF, at least in the sky you could only hit a fucking cloud.'

'Sorry John,' says I, knowing that anything more would only fuel the bastard.

'Yeah sure, sorry isn't good enough, it's too late for sorry,' he replied, his neck tightening like a turkey's at Christmas.

The inspection continued. John decided he'd remove the insurance disc and the tax disc and keep them safe. He then decided it would be better to give me the insurance disc, as I would need it for my replacement car. I breathed a sigh of relief. Replacement car. My execution was deferred.

All my personal belongings had been removed by my brother, the interfering bastard, the day before, and were being held at home, where I was still residing by the skin of my teeth. I checked the boot to see if all the important things were in place and, to my horror, discovered that the spare wheel was missing, though I diverted John's attention from this discovery, not wanting him to reverse his decision and execute me there on the spot.

The spare wheel is an important piece of equipment. Not only is it useful when one of the main wheels goes flat, but it also provides a very useful hiding place for items a man wouldn't normally want to be the subject of public viewing. My wheel was missing and my hiding place uncovered. I cringed with the realisation that that mean, penny-pinching, twisted, Ebenezer Scrooge bastard of a brother of mine had lifted the spare wheel and, with it, my personals. I knew now that there was more than one case conference taking place.

Sex was a dirty word, the act of sex even dirtier. Worse than dirt, it was sinful. Worse than that, it was a mortal sin. I was dirty, and now they knew. They'd known anyway, but now they had the evidence. I began to feel fucked again. I looked at John, thought of the mother, the brother, the whole lot of them, and I wished them all a roaring death in hell. At least I felt a bit better then.

We went to John's house, for what reason I don't know. I think he just wanted to show off, and indeed he had something to show. John's house was new, but built to look old – all the rage at the time. The fact that he couldn't afford it had nothing to do with it. We went into his hall, a big hall, like the one that was in the orphanage in Dominic Street, with high ceilings of moulded plaster, a throw-back to Georgian times.

'I'll put this in here,' said John looking at me as he opened his hall table drawer. He placed the said tax disc in it.

'Fine,' says I, afraid to utter more than one word at a time.

John introduced me to his wife, and a lovely wife she was too.

I don't think I would have had any problem if she had seen my personals, and better still if we had seen them together. I started to fantasise about taking her from behind as John watched, but John spoiled it by putting his hand inside his pants and I felt sick instead.

John dropped me to a car rental place and told me that Tony, a decent fella, would supply me with a car for my needs. Whether John lost his mind or what, I don't know. Certainly something happened, because his memory got fucked. My car was eventually fixed and back on the road – minus the tax disc. I rang John and, in a courteous manner, for I am a courteous kind of fella, I asked to meet him so he could give me the disc, which was snugly resting in his hall table.

'Yeah sure, don't tell me you lost the disc,' I heard him say down the line. 'I never took your tax disc or any other disc for that matter,' he said, lying through the base of his bollocks.

'You did, John,' I told him, making matters worse, for to question God is to die.

'Yeah sure, we'll see about that,' said John in his usual intimidating manner, full of threat and innuendo. I thought of going on the piss and saying fuck the lot of them, but decided not to, because I was at a stage when it was easier to stay off the drink than go on it.

The post arrived about a week later, and in it was a replacement tax disc. There was a letter of warning as well. One more misdemeanour and I was gone. If I do something wrong, no matter how small, I can live with the punishment, even if the punishment far outweighs the crime. But when I'm right – in fact when I'm neither right nor wrong because I wasn't even involved – and I'm blamed, it kills me. I begin to hate and despise whoever is involved and curse them to the high heavens. John was quickly reaching a position where he would depose the brother, and become the new No. 1 on my hit list.

The daily toil continued unabated, and I worked tirelessly for the greater good of the sweet and candy company. I hadn't any choice, the dole queues were full, the country was in mess and the company knew it. They used and abused their employees and got away with it.

Management by intimidation is a terrible thing. There is no possibility of looking forward to going to work, where everyone spends at least eight hours of every weekday. I remember the time when, one evening coming back from Cork, I felt like farting and instead I shit my pants. I spent a full hour hatching my own shit, as I drove home to change my clothes, before I could resume my work building the profits of the shareholders and investors of the sweet factory. God bless them all!

Nuisance Calls

My mother professed to love me, but betrayal was the only thing that she ever showed me. Everything she did, she did in love – or so she said. My definition of love is clearly quite different to that of my mother. Maybe hers was a tough kind of love, I don't know. I have tried to analyse it all my life, but I have never understood. The bond between mother and child is supposed to be the strongest possible. I often think of that line in the bible: does a mother forget her child or a woman the child within her womb? I don't think my mother forgot me. She did her duty, but there is a stark difference between love and duty.

I can't blame my mother for being pissed off when she was getting the nuisance phonecalls, but, in the name of all that's holy, it wasn't me that was making them. One way or the other, though, I was blamed, and – guess what? – I was thrown out yet again.

Anyone that has ever been the unfortunate recipient of nuisance phonecalls – and I've had a few myself from time to time – will know that they are a bastard to contend with. However, I'm not sure if the problem was just the nuisance calls or if it was the new girlfriend, or a combination of both, but the mother never approved of Herself, and she probably never will. It isn't as if my mother would be the one living with her, anyway, and the totally amazing thing is that she even cared. She had thrown me out on the streets so often that it was plainly obvious that she wasn't my number one fan. You'd have thought she'd be glad to get rid of me!

I came home one morning to remove about forty boxes of after-dinner mints from the lounge – formerly the garage and converted privately because it was cheaper. John had instructed me to sell the mints to a local supermarket. I had just commenced loading the car when the mother of all sorrows appeared before me in a beautiful pink towelling dressing-gown, covering the nightie, accompanied by a stunning pair of woolly socks and toeless slippers.

'You have to go,' she sobbed, 'you have to leave us in peace. I can't take any more,' says she, as if I was the reincarnation of Jack the Ripper and she my next victim.

'Ah go fuck yourself, you miserable oul' bitch,' I roared. 'If you want me to go, I'll go. I won't stay where I'm not wanted,' I thundered on, determined not to leave without getting my pound of flesh.

'Just go,' she cried – the snot was dripping into her mouth as she cried bitterly, pretending that she possessed a heart and everything was my fault. She was messing around with my head and I knew it.

I finished packing the car and, slamming the door behind me, I roared back at her, 'I'll be back later to take my stuff and this time I won't be back.' As if she gave a damn one way or the other.

Condoms Galore

That evening I arrived at my girlfriend's house all forlorn and in need of love. She lived with her mother in a four-bedroomed detached house in an almost rural area. Her father was dead, and she an only child. I imparted to my love my state of distress and she, not being a fan of the mother, was only too willing to oblige and showed me to my room. Things were looking up.

When I was a down-and-out and sleeping rough and, indeed, throughout other hardships, the hunger was the most unbearable aspect to be endured. As long as restaurants, take-aways and shops are open, money is in my pocket and at least four hours has passed since my last meal, I have got to eat. I am a well-known man in many varied and diverse eating houses and long may it last. While returning from one such culinary outing in my preferred chipper of the time, Herself gave a kind of muffled squeak as we approached her house under the cover of darkness. Alarmed, and concerned for her health as well as her state of mind, I turned my attention towards my love – who was also my landlady, if not in name, certainly in practice. She was pointing, however, at something outside the car and her beautiful mouth was hanging open in a most distasteful fashion. When my vision cleared, I too let out what can only be described as an insane shriek. There before me, on the road, neatly tucked against the wall of her house was my brother's car, all washed and shiny.

'Oh, mother of the divine Jesus, what in the hell is going on here?' said I, a feeling of impending doom enveloping my very being.

'Will we go in or what?' said Herself, displaying uncharacteristic cowardice.

'Jesus, we'll have to go in, your mother is in there on her own,' said I, making it look as if I was concerned for her mother's safety at the hands of my maniac family. In reality I was far more concerned about my safety and the security of my sleeping arrangements than I was about anything else. Those bastards could be telling her anything.

'It's true,' said Herself, 'we'll go in.' I parked the car in my usual spot to the left of centre and took a deep breath.

The sight that greeted us as we entered the bungalow I will never forget. The sitting-room, which was just inside the main door, had a glass-panelled door leading into it which, although closed, allowed the gravity of the situation to unfold. It wasn't a casual visit but, rather, a delegation. My family were there on a mission.

My girlfriend's mother sat on the corner of her seat, face ashen, unable to move. She was under attack. My mother, brother and sister were lined up on the couch, like three military judges at a courtmartial.

'What in the name of almighty fuck is going on here?' I asked in the voice of British aristocracy, as I opened the door and entered followed by Herself, who was visibly shocked and alarmed.

Herself's mother was clearly glad to see us and regained some composure, even smiling a timid smile.

'We have just been telling Maeve about the phonecalls we have been getting,' the mother began, obviously well warmed up and a far cry from the helpless defeated little woman who had ejected me from the house a few weeks earlier. 'We can't take any more and it has got to stop,' she continued, relishing her success in confronting her problem. You'd swear she had just completed a course on victim support.

'Have you now?' says I. 'And what the fuck has it got to do with Maeve?'

'Now, now,' the brother corrected me. 'There's no call for foul language in the presence of ladies,' he said, trying to bring me down to size.

'Ah fuck yourself!' said I. 'The only lady here is you, you sleazy bastard.'

'Sit down,' said Maeve quietly, almost pleading. As it was her house, I sat down. Christ, here I was again. I was only going out with a girl a few weeks and already a deputation of my fucked up relations had arrived to screw it all up as best they possibly could. I sat and waited, Herself beside me, and then the mother started her speech. I must say, that, even though it was about me – and not exactly an appreciation of my life to date – she delivered it well. She was always good at the art of speech making.

'Peter, you've broken our hearts. From the hour you were born you never gave me a moment's peace. That's all I've ever asked for, peace. Peace at any price. A bucket of peace. I had a tough life and I don't deserve for it to be any tougher. My mother died when I was young. I raised my brothers and my sister. I baked brown bread before I went to school. You may say that many a morning I drew water from the well, barefoot and hungry. My father beat me – with a ten-holed chain he beat me – and, Maeve, I always respected him. To this day I respect him. I'm a grown woman and I wouldn't speak to my father the way that pup has spoken to me. If I did I'd get the back of his hand. He has no respect for God nor man. Anyone that can speak to their mother like he has spoken to me is no good. You'll rot in hell and your own children will do to you what you did to me. Remember my words. Be warned. He's a bad egg.' I had to interrupt. She was on

107

a roll, but I had to stop her. It was a pity really, because I was nearly beginning to enjoy it myself. Shakespeare couldn't have done as well.

'Ah, shut your cake-hole, you oul' hag,' I roared over her voice.

'That's what I'm talking about!' she shouted in triumph, waving a clenched fist at me and turning back to Maeve. 'That's the scut I reared. Well, I'll be responsible for him no more! He'll have your daughter pregnant yet,' she revealed. I cringed in my seat. What was coming next? Oh sweet suffering and divine Jesus, why me? Why was I to be tortured like this? In my head I was beginning to sound like my mother, so I told myself to shut up.

'Tell her!' said the mother, looking towards the brother. 'Tell her what you found in his car when you kindly went out to help, and what way you were treated for that help – the offence you had to suffer. Tell her!' the mother roared. 'Tell her and be done with it, man. Tell her what you found under the spare wheel. Under the spare wheel! I ask you, Jesus, to deliver me this night. Tell her!' she roared again.

'Condoms,' says the brother, my peer, my dirty filthy two-faced bastard of a brother.

'Condoms! And not just ordinary condoms, but mint green ones that he can use on your daughter,' the mother roared, as if she were running for election against Ian Paisley.

Oh Christ, the embarrassment! I looked at Herself, who was by now white with shock. I then looked at Maeve, who looked as if she didn't know whether to laugh or cry. However, the brother wasn't finished yet. The bastard never is.

'He's not a virgin, you know, Maeve,' he revealed, the stupid unmerciful bastard. 'He's had sexual relations before. It's common knowledge. We feel it's best that you know and that your daughter takes measures to protect herself. You never know what she might catch.' Oh, sweet Jesus, I ask you!

Herself had had enough. She erupted.

'Get the fuck out of my house, you sick perverted bastard.' Good on you, love! Go for it! 'Doesn't everyone know about you and your behaviour,' Whatever that was supposed to mean I don't know, I don't think she knew herself, but it sounded good. 'If you think that I'm going to sit in my own home and listen to you talk about me in such a perverted way, you have another think coming. Now fuck off, the lot of ye.' That's my girl.

The three of them didn't know what had hit them. The sister had sat in silence, and I imagine she was giving thanks that she had. They had thought the inevitable would happen: Maeve would express shock and take a valium. When she felt better she would come back and tell me to get the hell out of her sight and never return. Herself would look at me in horror and see a beast, the image and likeness of Lucifer, and run into the waiting arms of my brother – seeking protection in his virginal embrace – and live happily ever after. This time they had got it very wrong.

Systems

Things of beauty have always appealed to me. Purity mingled with beauty appeals even more. In everything I did, I measured the beauty and went for the best. Standards rise with wealth, but the measure stays the same. Only that which is being measured differs. This is true for almost everything, save alcohol. It remains constant, never changing, old being best.

Water is my other great love. I am lucky to be a native of a riverland, and I revel in its beauty. Its purity may be lost, but I love it none the less. I often stand between the two bridges in the centre of my city and watch the water, sometimes still, other times angry, but always beautiful.

Current meets tide, waves dance.
Layer covers layer, bubbles kiss.
Pushing together, all the same,
Till stillness falls and all is calm.

Slowly first, it starts to flow.
Deep and dark, with grace it goes.
Faster then and faster still.

Till white water goes roaring down.
Water is peace, freedom and life.

The Curragower Falls, the last on the Shannon, epitomise everything good and bad in the life I have lived. The best of all is that moment when the tide settles, its conquest complete, peace envelops everything and the silence is deafening. At that moment the river is at its climax and resting a while. That is the state I have been seeking for as long as I can remember. I have, of course, sometimes found it, but, like my river, I have lost it again, and the search begins all over again, always moving further away before starting to return.

Ireland is a treasure of waterways, large, small and often unnoticed. I notice them all.

Tiny rivers, minute streams, ponds full of lily.
Coves in the sea, beaches hidden in rock covered by grass.
Lakes long and wide, locks small and deep.
All meet and mingle with me.

I found a climax one weekend in the purity of Mayo, resting in beauty. I can still close my eyes and see the dark redness of the water, the lushness of the grass and the soft unstoppable rain warmly caressing my face. Herself, who was then my fiancée, sat on the grass, my green umbrella protecting her as she smiled in silence, unaware of my peace. Small trout came to the fly, eels came to the worm and Herself took a trout, only to lose it again with the excitement of its arrival.

That night we dined together, the August sun falling behind Croagh Patrick as culinary delights entertained us, until finally we entertained each other. Lying in bed, smoking and drinking water, I blew smoke rings at the ceiling as the peace of the day settled me. However, I remained unaware that the urgency had gone. I fell asleep – Herself was already there – and dreamed happy dreams.

The following morning I went for a walk, Herself went shopping and all was well. The day was sunny but cooler than before, and the north wind was blowing. Westport House, set among trees and surrounded by water, sparkled in the sun as children played their happy games. Thoughts of the journey later in the day remained but thoughts, and thoughts of work and family were nowhere to be found. I returned to my room at the hotel. A note lay beside the phone – and the tide was on the turn.

'Ring John – urgently' the note said. I sat on the bed and my thoughts raced. I was on holiday, with still a week to go, and I was at peace. I debated if I really needed to ring him, but was afraid not to. Fear had returned and I wondered why. Herself came back and, always pragmatic, she said I should, so I lifted the phone.

The tide was gushing over the falls and into the estuary beyond. John was playing and the game was real. He told me that when I returned from my holiday I was being transferred. I was going to Cork. Over my dead body! This was about survival again, and I was going to survive. I wasn't going to Cork and I told him so, and to hell with the consequences. But the fear was frightening. The anger eventually came to my aid and I became normal once more.

I once read an interesting account of how a man saw his life improve when he learned of acceptance; that acceptance was the key to peace. In the article, as far as I recall, he said that, once he could accept that things were the way they were for a good reason and that nothing happens in God's world by mistake, then he found happiness. Good luck to him! I, on the other hand, could never accept that things have to stay the way they are. We make our own luck. I am not responsible for the badness of others, even though I have been the beneficiary of it once too often, but I have learned to fight my own corner and defend my right to happiness.

In a strange way the fight in me is always positive, but it is also always shadowed by fear. To quell that fear in times of threat I think of the streets and know where I've been. I have been low – couldn't go any lower – so let the world do its worst. I may not like it, but by Christ I'd survive it.

I didn't go to Cork. John made life hell for me and I had to look for another job. I had been looking anyway, but now I had to find one. I was offered a job with what I later discovered were a shower of total scumbags. John was tough, even ruthless, but he had some principles. I took the job and waved John goodbye. My first morning on the new job I was handed the phone book and told to look for insurance quotes. I knew then that I was up the creek.

The second and third day I spent on the Dublin Mountains modelling clothes for a new health and safety catalogue. It was the first time I actually believed that I might be good-looking. The fourth day I got the insurance and the car – and a disclaimer to sign that I would never claim copyrights for my modelling.

I stayed with this crowd for three months and then got the sack. That was a brutal blow and I took it bad. Getting the sack didn't just mean no money – the money was crap anyway – but it did mean no car, and that was serious. That night I returned from Dublin broken and, having suffered the indignity of public transport, I called on Herself. I had rented a room a long time since and needed to get back; tired from my ordeal, I needed sleep. I asked Herself to drive me home, but her mother refused to give her the car. One blow followed another. I got a hackney home.

A vampire can't come into the light, but, if an impenetrable cloak could be provided, I'm sure he would. I was like a vampire, my car my cloak. Without it I was naked. Fear prevented me from drinking. Things were bad and drink would only make them worse.

However, my friends said they'd help and they did. It was November; Christmas was coming. When a man is out of work and down on his luck; people usually run a mile. My grand-mother, a wonderful lady not unused to trouble, always used to say: 'Laugh and the world laughs with you. Cry and you cry alone.'

To be familiar with trouble is not necessarily a good thing. Experience of past difficulties can either strengthen or weaken a man. To know the manner in which people view failure, having sat with the successful, can diminish one's resolve. It took all my strength not to fold. I was on foot, without my own transport, and it felt as if everyone was looking, whispering, jeering, knowing. In hindsight, I know that people are too wrapped up in themselves to notice other people's problems. And after all, I know now that it really doesn't matter what people think. I decided to split with Herself. I felt that she would only want me if I was on top, that image was important. I was wrong about that as well.

Christmas that year was a disaster. I had had three interviews and it had been strongly hinted that I was the man for the job. The company was good, big and strong. I wanted the job and the dream kept me sane. I don't think I could have stayed off the drink except that there was something to look forward to. I was alone and crying in the dark. I isolated myself but wanted someone of my own. Anyone would do. January came, and so did the call. I was to start on the 20th. The tension left me and was replaced by excitement – the result was the same.

I always recall with sadness an afternoon that I went shopping for shoes and a new suit the week prior to my date of commencement. I had been meeting a man who was much older than I, and who was also off the drink. He was well read, a bit of an artist and talked of fishing and guns with great knowledge. I liked him a lot. I spent many evenings in his company and greatly appreciated his support through those difficult times. I left a shoe shop on the main street and decided I'd go to a yuppie bar for my afternoon coffee. After all, I was soon to be working for one of the biggest names in the world. I met my friend as I walked up the street. On seeing my purchases and hearing the good news, he flipped, accusing me of sneering at him, which is something I would never have done. He even threatened to knife me, and eventually I walked away, leaving his anger to himself.

I spoke to this man on two occasions afterwards but only briefly, for his actions had destroyed our friendship. His bitterness had frightened me and I have often wondered if I actually did anything – other than just get on with my life – to annoy him. I don't think I did, but I learned a good lesson about trust. He did me a favour really.

With my success getting the job, being off the drink and generally being of good behaviour, I was lonely. I no longer had Herself for company and I needed to gather some approval. After all, I was achieving something at last – in the traditional way. I went back home. Blood is thicker than water, at least mine is anyway. I have a short memory when things are good; they have to be very bad before I re-employ history. I sought the approval of home and got it. I was starting to play ball and, anyway, I just wanted to belong.

Baby

I was the envy of every twenty to thirty year old in my locality. I had a better job than most of their fathers and I had a flash car also. I was on my way and I was doing it in style. With every success there comes an arrogance. It manifests itself in different ways and in my case I began to feel greater than some, equal to others but less than most. It was a huge improvement!

The maturity of my new employer was unique for its time and its industry. They didn't view people with suspicion, and responsibility and accountability were there for the taking. It was up to each man and woman to do their job well and management were there to assist, guide and support. They didn't see their role as controlling or critical. I was given all the freedom I needed and the attitude towards expenses was fair and comfortable. They insisted that I look after myself and good food and quality hotels became a common feature of normal living. They reaped the benefits of course. People went to work in comfort and peace and gave the best of themselves. It made sense. They were going to incur expense anyway. The sweet factory begrudged their employees any comfort at all. They made people feel that they should be sleeping in tents. The difference in morale was marked. Everyone in the sweet factory was always grumbling and going to union meetings. They lost more through lost productivity while people were fighting and arguing for better conditions than they would have if they had behaved like human beings and treated people with the respect and dignity to which they were entitled.

In my early days in the new job I stayed in hotels quite frequently. At first hotels can be fun, but after a while they become boring and monotonous. The nights become longer than if you are at home and, even for the most balanced of people, hotels are lonely. Because I was off the drink I rarely went near the bars. These were usually lined with solitary drinkers reading the paper or staring blankly into their beer. Most people killed the boredom this way and invariably, after several drinks, the barriers came down and conversation developed and the nights passed a little easier. I occasionally went in search of women, but I was never successful. I think I would probably have needed to read a manual of how to go about it in the first place. Confidence with the fairer sex was never my strong point.

I was bursting with energy and threw myself into the job. My confidence improved and my social skills developed. When I was wearing the corporate hat I was Jack the lad. I mixed with all levels in various organisations and I could hold my own. I never felt intimidated and unable to perform – I could do it in style and with confidence. My turnover developed and it seemed I could do nothing wrong. I was successful, arrogance took root and I started believing in myself. I don't think this was a bad thing entirely. The only problem was that, when I retired to my hotel and could no longer hide behind the power of my employer, I was back to square one – naked, vulnerable and afraid. The confidence and self-belief never transferred into my private life. The arrogance did, however. I think it was about then that I started to rationalise in favour of the drink. If I could be successful in my career then the years of condemnation and loathing were without foundation and the instruction of my mother and brother that I would never amount to anything became apparent for what it was – evil and wrong. I wanted to drink. I wanted to join my fellows in the hotel bars and chat the nights away while getting merry and happy. I wanted to approach women in nightclubs and shake off my inhibitions and become liberated in their bedrooms. I didn't, however. I repressed it and got angry in a private concealed way. I was already angry in this way – it just developed further and faster. I was lonely and full of energy. I was bursting at the seams. I did a lot of good things with this energy, but most of all I laid firm and unquestionable foundations in my career. My reputation has never been called into question. Unfortunately, even I had to stop working at some time in the night. Then I was left alone with myself and a surplus of energy and no way in which to release it.

*   *   *

I was lonely. I decided to give Herself a shout. She looked surprised to see me but happy. Her mother just looked. Three months is a long time to go without sex, especially when you're in the habit of getting it. We went for a drive, to catch up on the missing months. Up into the mountains we drove, chatting away like a couple of teenagers, and on to a familiar haunt that we used to frequent in times of carnal need.

The needs of the flesh must be met. I called on a friend once and asked him for the use of his bedroom while he and his friends, who were not friends of mine, watched television. The plan went well until myself and Herself had to leave. We went out into the room and all heads turned to look at us as if we were half mad. Herself got especially embarrassed and tried to make out it was all my idea, until she realised she was only making matters worse and we left. I was known as 'randy Mac' for some time after.

I had a good car at this point and the need to bum a bed wasn't as crucial. I would still prefer a bed, but beggars can't be choosers – and after three months I wasn't a chooser, whatever about anything else. I'll say no more than that it was a memorable trip to the mountains.

A few week's later Herself told me she was 'late'. I insisted on a test being done immediately. I think Herself was quite surprised with my apparent familiarity with such matters, but she didn't pry for fear she might discover something she didn't want to know.

We went into town and into the Family Planning Clinic. Herself was even brandishing a borrowed wedding ring. She came back out about half an hour later smiling from ear to ear, and I thanked God for his mercy. It wasn't that I didn't want a baby, but, even then, a baby outside of wedlock was not acceptable. People pretended it was, but everyone knew it wasn't.

Herself got into the car and she started laughing. The longer she laughed, the more she laughed. I thought she had lost it.

'What in the fuck are you laughing at?' says I, getting angry from the frustration of it all. She laughed more at that, and I began to get seriously annoyed. 'Answer me, for Christ's sake!'

'It was positive,' she laughed, and as if I didn't hear her the first time she said it again, this time almost choking on the words, for she was now laughing hysterically. 'It waaaas positiiiivve . . .'

I didn't know what to do, so I did what I thought I should do and started 'fucking' and 'blinding' like a true blue bastard.

My world – which was just beginning to come together – began to fall apart. I didn't know what to say and the pressure of responsibility was immense. My mother had given me a complex about the dirty thing hanging between my legs. I can still see her as she told myself and the brother about the bold boys that made innocent young girls pregnant and then ran away leaving the poor unfortunate girl holding the child. I used to imagine the road to Dublin and all the bold boys hitching a lift, satchel on back, fag in mouth and legs shaking with the nerves. I was convinced that it was all the boy's fault and that the act of sex was a dirty despicable thing which girls had to endure because it was their duty to the filthy men. I remember feeling very relieved when I discovered that this was not, in fact, the case and that girls probably enjoy sex as much as any boy.

She was pregnant and that was that. I got the shits. Most people going through trauma use some sort of drug. My reaction was to smoke too much, get a migraine and a serious dose of the shits.

I told my mother the news and she wasn't impressed. The baby wasn't mine and there was no more to it. I didn't know how to take this. Was she saying I wasn't capable or what? She gave me a lecture telling me to keep my pants up and that I was a bold and silly boy. I hadn't expected her to congratulate me.

I told Herself what the mother had said, and she lost the use of reason – she was good at that. I couldn't understand any of what was going on. We were to be the proud parents of a brand new baby, and all that was worrying her was my mother. My family threw me out for the last time, and I moved in with Herself and lost contact with home. They were banned by Herself, of course. I started thinking of drink again, I needed some kind of release. I didn't break for almost two years, but that's because I'm really a coward.

I was always responsible. I knew what was expected of me and I did it – and more besides. There are no medals for doing what you're supposed to do. It was my duty to look after my woman and my unborn child, and I did.

The job was going well, and I was made permanent. I got the letter within six months, not like the sweet factory shower of bastards who extended the probation period for another three months. However, this crowd weren't into that kind of intimidation. All told, things were really pretty good. My woman was pregnant and I had a good job. Unfortunately, the job didn't pay very well. It wasn't bad for my age, it was just bad if a fella had a woman pregnant and she not earning herself.

I decided to celebrate and brought Herself to Scotland. She

brought a tenner. It was a great holiday. We toured the west coast and went down into Rob Roy country. They were like ourselves, the Scots – pure Celts – and I felt at home. Their police disappointed me. I think they had to pretend they were better than their English colleagues. It's a bit like meeting an Irishman in London, who, if he knows you're a republican, will hate you – unless he is one himself of course. He has to make out that he's a better Englishman than the English themselves. Even though he's Irish, he's ashamed to admit it.

It's understandable, though, if it's an Irishman in England, but a Scottish man in Scotland: that's a mind-fuck. I've heard it said that members of the RIC, before independence, were the very same to their own. If that's the case – and I have no reason to say it is or it isn't – I can only attribute it to the evil influence of the Queen. That being the case, I have to absolve all and sundry here and now, because this republican committed the same crime when stuck for porter money and in desperate need of a few pictures of the Queen to quench his thirst. Birds of a feather must flock together.

At any rate, the Scottish cops stopped us at Stranraer, when we were disembarking from the boat which had brought us from Larne in Northern Ireland. We were the only car with a Republic of Ireland registration. All the rest were either English, Scottish or, of course, Northern Irish. We were searched, even though there was no good reason for it. Herself was a nervous wreck, knowing my beliefs. She had no need to be, because the only gun I'd ever had had already been fired – and she knew all about that. Anyway, while I may sometimes look for a rush in some madcap kind of way, carrying arms across the Irish Sea is a bit too much even for me.

I met a Scot in a hotel in Colander on our way home. I make the point that he was a Scot, because I discovered there were a lot of English in Scotland as well. He educated me well on Scotland's problems and the Anglicised clan chiefs. The Brits always had a policy of divide and conquer and they did a good job in Scotland, but they failed completely in Ireland – they'll never do it to us. Maybe we're a purer breed of Celt. However, pure breeds have their weaknesses, and no prizes for guessing what ours is.

All in all it was the best holiday I ever had. When we arrived back in Ireland I was fairly skint. I stopped at a petrol station and asked Herself to buy me a packet of fags out of her incubating tenner. She told me to fuck off – and the tide was going out again.

Power Lost

I lived with Herself and her mother for most of the statutory nine months. I got well into the job, and stayed away from home a lot. My family would occasionally come on the scene, but an argument would quickly flare up and then I'd have to listen to it for weeks afterwards. To be fair, they messed with her head. The girl was young, pregnant and living with her mother and me. She had enough to deal with, but I soon started to hate the lot of them.

Weakness is a terrible thing, and they had made me weak. I was weak in a cowardly way. I was afraid of the consequences of tough action. If I had asserted myself then, I might have been spared a lot of torment, I might even have gone a different route. I didn't – I hid instead.

The pull of a pint and its settlement is a beautiful thing. The thirstier and the more in need of it a man is, the greater the beauty. I can't say the same beauty exists with lager, but it has its own frothy attraction, in a wild and turbulent sort of way. It is more reminiscent of rough seas, rather than the quiet solitude of the lagoon. To a drinking man like myself, the pint of Guinness is the purest form of pleasure. It can't be rushed and time is an important ingredient for its enjoyment. Lager is a party drink, sloppy and informal. It can go anywhere and do anything, but it's not a man's drink and should never be confused with such. It is, of course, often drunk by men, but only if an aforementioned party is imminent. The mixing of drinks is strictly not recommended. Guinness is the unrivalled champion of true beauty.

Herself woke me at five in the morning and told me that the birth of my child was soon to take place. She went back to her room and proceeded to pack. We weren't married, so sleeping in the same bed was a sin, against all good Catholic beliefs. The fact that she was up the spout, and my noble spout at that, didn't make a difference. I hadn't argued. I was glad of the bed, and even happier about the roof. I received the occasional visit and, God bless her mother, she is a sound sleeper.

The sick members of our extended community – namely my own family – were of course convinced that we were sleeping together. Their simple little minds were even prepared to suggest that I was probably servicing Herself's mother as well. The truth of it is that Herself's mother is a model widow. Her husband had died and that was that – I have never seen her with a man.

I love the bed. I always did, but since sleeping rough I love it even more. A good night's sleep is everything and I'm not a man for burning the midnight oil. To be woken out of a fitful sleep at five in the morning is not high on my list of pleasurable experiences. Herself came back into the room to see if I was dressed and, sure, I had returned to dreamland and a lovely black-haired beauty was there with me. The first fight of the day took place even before I got out of the bed.

We drove to the maternity hospital, and we were lucky enough to see a fox on the way there. It was the first time I had ever seen a fox in suburbia, and I'm delighted to say it happened that morning.

Herself lay on the hospital bed in the labour ward, her legs in stirrups, and I just looked on helplessly. She started to abuse me towards the end, but I didn't mind, being used to it. It was just a bit embarrassing in front of strangers. The labour went on all morning and I was never so glad that I wasn't a woman, after what I saw that morning.

The final push, and a little black head appeared. The head on Guinness is white. Then the body appeared, two-toned and not yet settled (also like Guinness). A wipe of a cloth and she was white (Guinness reversed). She was the most beautiful thing I had ever seen (after the pint). The November midday sun shone through the windows and bounced off the child and my blood-stained white shirt. The midwife placed her in an incubator and Herself and I both looked at her, wondering if she was really ours. She was the tiniest thing I had ever seen.

Then I held her. Nothing can compare to that moment – not even Guinness. Small and helpless, she looked up at me, her warm body in constant motion, and I felt the love. She was the most beautiful thing I had ever held and she was mine. I felt I belonged for the first time in my life. She became the purpose of my life and from that moment she determined my existence. She took my power and I gave it willingly. She was to give it back to me later in plenty – in order to save me. I love her very much.

Marriage

We had to get married. Society demanded it. We were living together, had a baby, slept in different rooms – and her mother was there. My crowd were nice one day and causing trouble the next. They told me that I was a victim and they told Herself that I was a bastard. I didn't know what I was.

The baby was great and everyone loved her. I got on with life and did my best to meet my new responsibilities. I felt like a drink, but I didn't drink. I measured up and kept everyone happy. Herself, her mother, her relations and I pandered to my family, hoping they'd let me belong, but they didn't. They just kept me in the cold, hanging me out when they felt like it. I gave them the ammunition, of course. I should have known better, and in many ways I did, but I wanted them to change and so I gave them every opportunity.

Massive debates ensued in my head. I needed an outlet, and drink seemed to be the obvious one. I laid it out logically. My family behaved badly and I did what I did because of them. Everything bad that I had happened had been as a reaction to them or caused by them. Logic said drink. My fear said don't, and so did my friends, and both of these kept me off it.

But still I fought it and didn't drink. I stayed close to my friends and they said 'accept'. Silently I cursed them, and I tried to accept.

We set the date and laid the plans. The wedding was great. Herself looked fantastic – she opened a few mouths. I looked good as well. My best man was my best friend. I had asked the brother, thinking yet again that if I was nice to him he'd be nice to me. He might even want to be my friend. But I was disappointed yet again. They all came, however, the old lady and all. Some of her family from the country came as well and I was delighted, as I like them a lot.

The day went well; everyone said it was the best wedding they were ever at. I can't say the same thing myself, but then I don't like weddings. I didn't drink, but nobody expected me to. The only hiccup was the mother. The wife and myself were just about to go and consummate the union when my old lady appeared. She threw her arms around the wife and said, 'I'll accept you, so, your faults and all.' I was to hear about that for the next six months. What am I talking about? I'm still hearing about it!

We went to Greece for the holiday. It was supposed to be a honeymoon, but from what I've heard about honeymoons it certainly wasn't one. We arrived at Rhodes, a total disaster of a place. I christened the place we were staying 'Walton's Mountains – the Missing Years'. The brochure said the place was a Lotuseater's paradise, which was a reference to the lush beautiful vegetation, I'm sure. But the only thing the bastards ate was me!

It was a poverty-stricken kip. It was like winding the clock back thirty years and finding yourself in any Irish village on the western seaboard. That stuff may appeal to the Americans, but it certainly doesn't do anything for me. I had my own share of hardship and I'm not inclined to sit and watch some Greek bastard having his.

The beach was two miles away; a 'leisurely stroll' the brochure said. Since getting a car I walked nowhere. I did all my walking in the first twenty years of my life and it's a poor man's pastime. I decided to rent a motorbike but couldn't afford a good one, so I got a Honda 50 instead. It was a grand bike, except when we were going up a hill the wife had to walk.

We toured the island and saw it all. Mind you, there wasn't a lot to see. One thing was obvious though: the Brits, the Dutch and the Germans had all the nice spots – what there was of them.

It's typical of course. The Paddy is always thrown into the second-class rubbish. It wasn't the fault of the Greeks or of any of the other aforementioned nationalities – with the possible exception of the Brits of course. The Irish always screw their own; it's part of the national condition. We have the greatest inferiority complex of any nation, and the only ones to blame are ourselves. The Brits may have done it to us, but we allowed them. They're talking about peace now, but the Brits need to do some apologising, as far as I can see. It's not going to happen of course. Eight hundred years of tyranny, rape, murder and persecution comes nowhere near a few bombs within the Queen's ear shot.

The wife wanted to party. In fairness to her she can party. I've seen her drink many a good man under the table, myself included. A boring, non-drinking husband wasn't the best company at half past darkness, when the cocktails were flowing and she was feeling no pain. We had a couple of fights and she said she was going home to her mother. With the amount of topless women about I was beginning to hope she would.

We met a couple from Macroom in County Cork, who were great fun and liked to party as well. The wife got on well with them and they spent their evenings in a local pub on the razz. My past was discussed at length, the conclusion the same as before – I was right, the family were wrong. I agonised, but I didn't drink.

After about a week I wanted to go home. The swimming was hopeless as well. The beach was on the edge of a shipping lane and Turkey wasn't too far away. The water was a mixture of oil and Greek and Turkish shit, which is about all the mingling these bastards do. Even the Brits and ourselves are more civil to each other – in the absence of the odd gun or two of course.

I was in Paris a number of years later at a company weekend. We were taken to a show and some genius decided it would be good for the harmonisation of the European Community if the Greek National Sales Manager and the Turkish equivalent would sit opposite each other. I was at the same table as these two, with a sound character from Belgium. The Greek and the Turk sat at the end of the table and neither looked at each other, nor anyone else for that matter, for the entire evening. The Belgian and myself thought it was great fun, and we even had a solitary Brit to hassle as well.

I was very tanned and it was the last day of the honeymoon. The wife was brown as well, but not like me. She's a natural redhead, and therefore fair-skinned. I've brown hair and a sallow complexion. When I was young I thought my skin colouring was the answer to a lot of questions. I had decided that I was either adopted or the result of an indiscretion. The latter was discounted as quickly as it was thought of. The adoption route seemed the most likely, even though my mother also has brown eyes. I used to search through various papers I found hidden in the folks' bedroom in an attempt to discover my true identity. I never did, but I felt different anyway. I just didn't belong.

A black fellow came to our school when I was thirteen. A black man in Ireland is a very rare thing indeed. I became his friend. He was a Nigerian, from Lagos, and his family had sent him and his brother and some cousins to Ireland for the education. We didn't have much, but we had education. He was a nice enough fellow but could sometimes be a bit insincere. I hung around with him just because he was different; when I was with him I didn't feel so different. My mother of course hated him, devout Catholic that she was. After all, he was black. I thought that was strange, because her favourite saint was St. Martin De Pores, and he was as black as the ace of spades, God bless him. I started to resemble my father as I got older and I had to forget about the adoption hypothesis. I had to settle for the black sheep theory instead.

We had to wait until the middle of the night before we could fly home. The cheapskate travel agents exploited us in every way possible. I've never been on a holiday since. Once home, I drove straight to the west, and when I reached the ocean I jumped in and swam out off the head. There I floated until my brown turned to blue and I had to go home.

Drudgery

Marriage changes everything. It's no longer 'can I have a ten-ner', it's 'give me a tenner'. And there are no more blow jobs either. I adjusted very easily. After all, I had been living with her anyway, I just had someone in the bed now – officially at any rate. The sex didn't come as often, even though we had no sneak-ing around to do. Once it's legal it isn't the same.

I was living in someone else's house, so I kept my mouth shut – and paid all the bills. The wife and her mother had a great time. They played house, raising baby and all that, and I went to work. When I wasn't at work I did the lawn, cut the hedges and cleaned out the garage. When they went out drinking I drove, and if they didn't want me with them I did the babysitting. One way or the other, they did as they liked and I did as I was told. The mother-in-law even made me take out life insurance in case I died. I was only twenty-four and they wanted me to die!

When Pud had her first birthday, we had been married five months. We had a big party and I became very sick – my lungs felt as if they were on fire and I knew something was seriously wrong. They all sang happy birthday to the baby, drank Irish coffees and went off to the pub. I stayed at home and minded Pud, along with the wife's cousin's child – a lovely child.

Pud couldn't sleep and kept me up all night. My asthma was getting worse and I needed sleep. The wife, the mother-in-law and the cousin didn't come home until five in the morning and they were very pissed. I was pissed off.

'Where in the name of almighty fuck were you until this hour?' said I to the wife, adopting the role of the cross husband. Really I was just feeling close to death's door and in need of a doctor.

'Who the fuck do you think you're talking to?' said the mother-in-law, suddenly showing her face. It was obvious they had decided to pre-empt trouble, giving it before they got it. 'Tell him to get the fuck out of my house,' she said to the wife.

'You heard her,' said the wife. 'Get out!' Happy birthday, Pud, my arse!

I drove west through the pitch dark towards the coast. My lungs were getting worse and I wondered if I should go to the hospital. I decided I couldn't, because the wife and her mother would only say I was looking for sympathy and trying to make them feel bad. I met the guards on the way, at a checkpoint. They were trying to catch people driving while under the influence.

'Are you all right?' the cop asked me as he stuck his face in the window and down my throat to see if he could get a whiff of drink. I was under the influence all right, but not the sort he was looking for.

'The wife came in drunk and threw me out,' I replied.

'Drive on, so,' he said. 'You'll be grand.'

The Irish guards are very well trained. I drove on to the coast, parked the car, tried to breathe and got some sleep.

I slept until 9.30, when a guard tapped at the window and woke me. A guard is never around when you want one.

'You have to move on out of here,' said he in a guard-like tone of voice. The wind was howling, the sea roaring, and not a sinner in sight and this useless prick was telling me to move on. 'There's no parking or camping here,' he continued. I was well used to his type. 'Move on now or I'll summons you.'

I know it's a terrible thing to say, but at times I wonder if we would have been better off if the revolution had never taken place. Good men died to give this moron the right to wear a uniform and hassle the ordinary man, instead of protecting old women and men in their homes and children from paedophiles. Fellows like this one spend their time hand-picking the easy target. And I was an easy target.

I started the car and drove away. I was feeling worse, but it was Saturday and I didn't want to go to hospital because the only one open was like a glorified veterinary clinic. It was the one where all the country people went. The city hospital was a grand spot – after two hours in there, the whole town would know where you were – whereas in the other place you could be dead and gone and nobody would even know you'd been sick. Sometimes it can be nice to be sick, because people are nice to you. I wanted people to be nice to me, and the more the merrier. I decided to go home and try my luck with the two tulips. It was an awful thing not to be able to go home, but I was well used to it. Although I never became immune, it doesn't hurt as much after it has happened a few times.

They were very hung over, dying the death of fourteen martyrs. Not only that, but they were very sorry for having thrown me out. Now, in my estimation, everyone can act badly – and they had acted badly in a big way – but if you're wrong and promptly admit it then it has to be forgotten about. To say sorry when you're sober and your crime is fresh takes a lot of guts. The apology had to be accepted. At any rate I was in no condition to do otherwise.

I took to the bed and was pampered. Then I got thick and decided I'd be a hero – I wouldn't let them call a doctor. It wasn't that I was being a hero really, I just wanted to get plenty of mileage out of their guilt. Eventually I collapsed and couldn't walk, so the wife rang the doctor anyway. The doctor came and shipped me to the vets. However, they were full so they shipped me to the city. It all worked out grand in the end.

Season of Goodwill

Christmas that year was a total disaster. We weren't talking to my family yet again. I can't remember what they'd done or what they'd said, but for certain they'd done something. The wife and her mother drank their loafs off and a Yank came from Chicago and they all drank their loafs off together. I sat there, because I didn't know what else to do.

I was a lot softer then than I am now. I'll fight my corner now, although I'd rather not have the fight in the first place. I was lonely without my crowd, it being Christmas, and I moaned on about them to anyone that would listen. They all said the same – 'Have a pint, can't you?' – but I didn't.

I stopped calling on my friends, because I thought they were having a bad influence on me. They were older than me anyway and had all done a lot of drinking and seen life. I couldn't relate to them any more, and anyway I didn't want to. But I was feeling under a lot of pressure and I was getting very pissed off. Life in Ireland revolves around the pub. It's a terrible thing for a non-drinker to have to cope with. You're always an outsider looking in.

I like fishing and swimming, even shooting, but I do these things mainly on my own. I like being alone, but it's nice sometimes to have company. The only place to get company was in the pub, so I started to go to the pub, just for the company. However, although the company was good I didn't belong. I never got invited to parties, but I was handy for a lift, so I was tolerated. The last thing a crowd of drinkers want is for some sober dry-balls to be sitting with them counting their drinks and generally showing them up.

Then Easter came and I couldn't take any more. I'm a good cook when I want to be, so I decided I'd cook the dinner for Easter Sunday. I bought the ingredients and a bottle of wine for the mother-in-law and the wife. They went off to the pub with the baby and told me they'd be back at two, but when the dinner was cooked they didn't come home. Two o'clock soon became four and I was angry. When the wife came home at four-thirty she was pissed. I abused her and she abused me back.

'Go away and drink for yourself and show that you're a man,' she yelled. 'Why can't you be normal and drink a pint like every other man?'

I looked at her and thought about it. It was what I'd been waiting for and I wasn't going to have her tell me twice. I had played ball with everyone but myself for almost four years. I had watched them drink and party all night on many a night. I had felt like a stranger in my own town and had been at everyone's beck and call. In short, I had allowed myself to become a doormat and I was sick to death of the whole goddamned thing. The simple fact was that, although I knew the drink wasn't the answer, I didn't have any defence against it. I felt as if I no longer had a choice, there was only one way to save my sanity and at the same time risk losing it. I got the wine, poured it out and drank it. It was done. I don't know who was more shocked – the wife or me. I poured another and drank that too.

'I'm going out now,' said I, 'and fuck the lot of ye!' I put on my coat and away I went.

Emancipation

Four years is a long time. I used to be able to drink a lot. I forgot that I no longer had any resistance, so it was like the first time all over again. The only difference was that this time I knew what was happening. I was like a leper leaving his colony, cleansed and cured. The burden of guilt and the feeling of difference lifted. I was recalled from the world of banished drinkers and rejoined the world of normal people.

I called a pint, a beautiful creamy pint the like of which I have never seen before or since. It was perfection of the highest order; it was the most perfect specimen even to come out of St. James's Gate. It was pulled with reverence and with the hand of experience. Exhilaration flowed through me and I licked my lips. My buttocks shifted and I drew closer to the bar, my hands joined, my breast leaning on the carved wooden handrail as beads of sweat lined up on my forehead and my balls moved.

The black pint tinged with red stood before me, capped in white, wholesome and full. I took the glass in my hand and, as if I had never left it, closed my eyes and brought it to my lips. Neck tilted, arm tilted, and back it flowed. My emancipation was complete. I placed it, half full, on the bar in front of me and studied it, experience telling me to wait, as I gathered up my shackles and threw them away. The tension gone, a peaceful ambience filled my senses. I felt I belonged. I knew I did.

I picked up the glass once again, drank the remainder, and then let the beautiful white head slide slowly down to the bottom of the glass. Then in one swift movement I threw it back, swallowing it whole. I beckoned the barman and called another. He filled it with ease, unaware of my long absence, and when it was ready passed it to me in the familiar way, taking the money from the change on the counter.

The ceremony that exists with Guinness drinking is a wonder. It is full of romance and rich thoughts. I have often felt a sorrow for my British neighbours, their bitter being as uncouth a drink as lager.

After six pints I was buckled. I got lonesome and the guilt came back. I was sorry that I was drinking and afraid of what might happen. I thought of Pud and decided to go. I called a taxi and a kind man helped me in. I didn't know what was happening to me. I had never before felt guilty when I had drink on me, only afterwards. I thought of everything that my friends had told me and I felt helpless and miserable. I finally arrived home and, after throwing up in the bathroom, went to bed, where I lay perfectly still as the room moved around me, restless and unrelenting.

I woke the following morning and felt awful. My head hurt and my mouth was like sawdust. I looked in the mirror and didn't like what I saw. My eyes were bloodshot and my mouth was stained with the stale darkness of Guinness. The sick was still in the toilet. I didn't feel so liberated then. I swore that that would be the last time and I meant it. I decided to call on my friends later, to tell them and start again. I decided that this would strengthen rather than weaken me. I cleaned up, had a shower and went back to bed. It was a bank holiday after all.

That night I went on the piss. I didn't get drunk as quickly and it was great. I went to my local pub and I was like a returned emigrant. I met a load of old cronies and we had a few good drinks.

The wife wasn't too happy. She was, by now, seriously doubting her wisdom that Easter Sunday, whereas I was delighted with myself and even started calling my breakout 'The Easter Rising'. I had something in common with 1916 after all. The pleading started, ultimatums and all, and I not two days back in the land of nod. I wasn't to come home drunk. I wasn't to open the door with my key. If I knocked on the window she'd let me in. She didn't want her mother to know. I thought this was all quite ridiculous. After all, Herself and the mother-in-law had been drinking for years. However, I wanted a quiet life and so I did as I was told. I never liked to go drinking in the middle of an argument – the drink is dear enough without the wife spoiling the buzz with her unholy torment.

I went out every night from then on. I waited until the mother-in-law went to bed – she always went about ten, God bless her – and then away with me. The local pub was owned by an absolute headbanger. If you so much as looked crooked at him, he'd be fit to stab you. Everyone ran from him, but I was happy to sit with him. He was my sort of man. I'm very good at appeasing maniacs. I'd had loads of practice with the brother.

The owner thought I was a grand fellow. He was partial to a few pints himself and was very generous also. Pubs in Ireland close at 11.30 p.m., which only left me less than an hour and a half to get in my quota, usually about eight pints or so. It wasn't a lot of time really, especially if a man got the inclination to have an extra one or two, the need being on him.

When the owner was drinking there was no problem; he was quite happy to stay back. After-hours are a great thing. An illegal pint is better than two legal ones, and I stayed back many a night. At this point I knew when I had enough, I was in control in a loose sort of way. When I wanted to leave, the owner would growl and, he being a big man, I didn't press the issue. No one went anywhere until he said so. I had more than the one or two extra drinks on many a night as a result.

I was getting annoyed at having to sneak around. A man

should be able to go in his own front door after a few pints. It wasn't my front door, of course, but that isn't the point. Whenever I could I stayed away with the job. The job was great, because I could stay in hotels and do what I liked and nobody knew a blessed thing. Many a good piss-up was had in the holy name of business. I was in deep by then and I decided I was there to stay.

The boss never said anything, but I'm sure he wondered. My expenses suddenly increased. My hotel receipts had drink bills that were never there before, and there were regularly receipts from various taverns around the country. All of a sudden I was one of the lads. Anyone looking on must have found it very entertaining.

Transformed

My entire social circle changed. I hadn't much of a social circle prior to this, but the little I had disappeared. The people I met when I was on the road changed also. I became great friends with all the reps that drank, and one in particular. He was a mad bastard – and he's still at it. The man can drink all day and all night. He can smoke eighty cigarettes in a day and drive the car when he's lallowed with sauce and no one says a blessed thing. He's my hero.

After two months, my transformation was complete. I was back on top and could drink Lough Éireann dry. Then the trouble started. The mother-in-law started acting the bitch, the wife was pregnant again and they had eased off the drink. Maybe they hadn't, but it certainly seemed like they had from where I was sitting.

The wife was giving me a hard time, but I had the perfect excuse – her mother. Mother-in-laws get an awful hard time and it really isn't fair. I had decided to be a hard man and even disappeared a couple of times. I didn't really, I just went to work and didn't say where I was going. It looked bad, however, and the mother-in-law bitched a little bit more. They were always nice when I came back – the war was put on hold.

Eventually I had to get out. The mother-in-law was killing me. She wanted her grass cut – and a day's drinking to be done. I had got fairly close to a friend of mine who knew the story and he provided the solution. He was living on his own, had left his partner, who just happened to be my wife's cousin.

'They're spoilt bitches,' he said. 'Never knew a day's want in their lives. They still think they're sailing on daddy's yacht!' He knew best, he was older after all.

I decided to leave and move in with him. The wife was devastated. The baby was one and a half, there was another on the way and I was leaving. The Irish divorce.

Himself and myself had a ball. We drank our loafs off and didn't give a shit. It was great. The wife would call round for a few bob and I'd give it. In fairness, I always gave it – I knew I should. I was living in a bachelor's paradise. My friend called Herself 'the queen' and all the lads were 'Maurice'. He introduced me to all the 'Maurices' and they were all hiding from their own queens. Things were looking up. He was part of a crew, a community, and all his family – who were well liked and respected – were there as well.

I began to feel I fitted in. The only lesson I had to learn was that pubs were full of liars, so I'd have to unlearn my habit of always telling the truth. I became known as a great liar and in many ways that wasn't a bad thing, because good liars were respected during drinking hours. I told the publican that I had rowed my boat – which in fact was more like a bathtub than a boat – into town one morning and that I had reached the town in less time than it taken a neighbour to drive there in his car because the traffic was so bad. I had seen the neighbour's car on the bridge as I rowed underneath. The publican thought this story was a great lie. He started talking about a river bus, and its captain. It was, in fact, the truth, but it was simply too real to be believed.

Property

My friend was lonely and eventually got back together with his queen. In fairness to him, it had probably seemed too good to last but it was great while it did. They decided to cut through the crap and get married.

His queen had her own house and they decided they would sell his, rent hers out and buy a bigger one. I decided that I'd buy his. The bank helped of course, and his queen worked in a bank, which helped as well.

I sent for my own queen and she came, baby and all, and the next one almost due. We were a family again – and no mother-in-law. We said we'd make a go of it. It wouldn't be easy, but we'd have a go anyway. Houses are great, but they take a lot of time to get right. While I was getting mine right, I stayed right. I eased off on the drink and Herself was happy. I just went to the pub where all the Maurices went a couple of times a week, I drank my fill and went home. Things were fairly normal. I was drinking with men and I was becoming a man – pub style. My queen didn't seem to mind so much; I think she even liked the new me.

Then the baby arrived. She was beautiful – and the image of

me. She was like the first baby born in freedom to an emancipated slave; the mother-in-law had no say. I rang the friend that I'd bought the house from and we went on the piss – I thought that was what real men do. I knew the queen would be pissed off, and the drink wasn't as good as it should have been, but we got buckled and met another Maurice and we all went back to my house. My friend had only been married a month, and I had been best man. It would all be my fault.

The following morning the shit hit the fan. The mother-in-law arrived first, sent by my queen to supervise the hanging of new curtains. Then the friend's queen arrived and all hell broke loose. The mother-in-law went straight to the hospital and told the wife. The other Maurice had disappeared, leaving the bed in a mess, which the mother-in-law assumed meant that I had had a floozy in it. My queen was told all of this and she started crying.

I don't like people to be upset, especially the queen. An unhappy queen is a nightmare. I felt very bad about everything and tried to make it up. I knew I was in the wrong, but that didn't make the mother-in-law right. The friend's queen had put in her tenpence worth as well. They'd all dropped me in the shit and I decided never to go on the piss again – it wasn't worth it. I'd go on best behaviour and change my ways. I succeeded for a while. The friend didn't really suit me anyway. He was a binge drinker and was too passionate with the glass – he couldn't get it in fast enough. He'd drink like crazy over a few days and then go off it for a while. I preferred the slow drink, long and peaceful. I liked it regular, like every night. I wasn't into being pissed, just nicely. When it was nicely, I was happy and everything was wonderful. When I was pissed I was an asshole, and half the time I couldn't even remember what I'd done. I didn't like that; it made me afraid. I drank to kill fear, not to feel it.

The queen came home from the hospital and so did the baby. It was nearly Christmas, so I wouldn't have to be good for too long. The baby was great and I got very close to her. I was close to the eldest as well, but so was the mother-in-law. The second one was all mine. She even looked like me: sallow skin and brown eyes. She was also very cuddly – a real little lady.

One Sunday I decided to go for a pint before lunch. I had never been into drinking during the day because when you stop you feel knackered for the rest of the day. When you start you need to stay at it. I brought the eldest, who was two now. I discovered that there was an entire culture surrounding Sunday lunchtime at the pub. I wondered why I hadn't thought of it earlier. Most people had gone to twelve o'clock mass first and then on to the pub. The next Sunday we went to mass as well.

The pub was a working-class one. I was more middle class but working class suited me better. All the Maurices went there as well. They all supported the same rugby team, so I became a rugby fan. I'm really a fisherman and didn't know anything about rugby, but that didn't matter, I was only there for the drink and so was everyone else. We just pretended to be interested in rugby. After all, people couldn't go into a pub and talk about alcoholism, they had to talk about something else, and sport is always a good option. It's a bit of a contradiction of course. They were talking about healthy pursuits on the field of play, while killing themselves slowly with booze. They didn't have the monopoly on that insanity, however.

The pub was small, forty foot long by sixteen wide. It was a real man's pub, with the occasional woman. It soon became my first home and I spent all my time there. The world is full of cliques and the people who frequented this pub were just another. I'd been on the outside too long and I was determined to belong somewhere. I became a fully fledged Maurice and a rugby fan. I even changed my accent. I called another pint and the emptiness continued.

I was very naïve. I really didn't have a clue and, despite all my experiences, I wasn't experienced at all. It was easy to fool me and easier still to make an impression on me. Most of the men I drank with were tradesmen – men of the world. They were all great drinkers. They knew every angle there was to know and had explored them all. If they hadn't they pretended they had and they were very convincing. The truth didn't exist. When I told the truth they thought I was telling lies. So I had to become a Maurice and be a liar like them – that's how I got in.

It was all innocent fun. It never went beyond the pub, and if it did it only went to another pub, and that was allowed. The queens were told nothing, or so I believed. I told mine nothing. Anyway, there wasn't much to tell.

I used to think that anyone that was fond of the drink was just a lost soul like myself. This meant they were nice and lovable but had a few problems. I discovered I was wrong. There are as many bastards drinking as there are who are not. A drinking bastard is a particularly evil one. He generally comes in with a packet of smiles and a firm handshake, but he has no principles and is utterly selfish. Drinking bastards are drawn from all walks of life, but they are frequently 'townies' and often guards. The guards have an extra angle. They have an appearance of being the bearers of knowledge, even if this is totally unfounded. This can work in their favour, but can also work against them. Ordinary fellas like me who had never done anything wrong were unsettled by the guards. After ten minutes in their company we were nearly inventing crimes to see if they would shag off and leave us alone.

I am from the city but I'm far from being a 'townie'. I'm a mixture of urban and rural. In a way I'm a farmer without a farm. I spent much of my childhood on the land with my grandfather and my uncles, where I experienced the richness of nature and the instinctive intelligence of animals. Once that richness of life and all things living has penetrated a man's soul, there is no return. However, I lived in a city and had to try to be urban. Fortunately, my city is not a large one and escape into nature is a simple thing. I visit Dublin, a big city by my standards, on a regular basis and I pity its inhabitants. To my mind there is no quality of life when you are surrounded by man-made structures. I have, of course, sometimes lived in big cities, but even when my body is caged my spirit is wild and free.

My friend that introduced me to all the 'Maurices' rarely showed up in the pub after the baby was born. His queen had him well shackled after his expedition into the land of unattached men. I drank with his friend, who was a blow-in Maurice like myself. He was a townie like the rest of them, but from a different part of town.

Rugby is a religion where I come from, and a man's class and his address denote the club he supports. The 'blow-in' was working-class and he grew up supporting a working-class club. This club has a reputation for passion. Once a member, always a member. The bastards would stab you for a kick of the ball. In the absence of a ball, they'd settle for a head, any head at that. The Maurice rugby club is upper working-class, breaking into middle class. It is centred in one particular parish, but its members are far flung. A lot of them are tradesmen, top notch, of course, but there are a doctor and a few solicitors to be found on close inspection. There were a lot of my type – the white-collar bullshitter.

The blow-in tried to stay faithful to his heritage, but he went to all the Maurice games and he drank with all the life-long Maurices. I think we stuck together because we both knew we didn't really belong – we looked better together than apart. But then again I'm not too sure about that either. He was a great drinker. He was the cute type: you never knew how much he had drunk. He always arrived in the pub at five-thirty or so and said he was just coming in after work. I believed him, but then I believed everyone. My queen saw him coming out of a pub in town in the middle of the afternoon one day, but when he met me later on he said he was looking forward to his first pint, having just finished work. He had everyone fooled, but you'd want to be a good Maurice to fool my queen. I was blatant, he wasn't; he could control it – that was the difference.

The blow-in and myself drank the evenings away talking about fishing and shooting. He fancied himself as a bit of a great white hunter, even though he didn't know how to hold a fishing-rod. He knew a bit about shooting, but I knew more. I never told him that though – there was some truths I wasn't naïve about.

The Peak

I reached my peak very quickly, and when I reached it I stayed there for a good while. If I could have stayed there, I'd still be drinking. I could drink what I liked and go home when I liked. Getting up for work was never a problem for me, and I never drank until after work, unless I was drinking while working and that was okay because it was allowed; that was business.

During my peak I never got hangovers, not the bad ones anyway. Every so often I'd get a good hangover, and they were like gold dust. A good hangover is a great thing – with it a man can drink all day and never get drunk. He just gets a buzz and stays on it for hours, and eventually falls asleep. The hangover from a good hangover is a total bastard. All the familiar friends come back – you feel as guilty as sin, you're afraid of your shite, you look like death and, if you're really unlucky, you'll have bleeding piles as well. This only applies to the nice guys, of course. The bad bastard deals with his demons in private.

To have a lot of money at a time like this is a bad thing. I'd go on a spending spree. Whatever the wife wanted she'd get. The kids as well. I'd try and buy myself out of the hole I'd dug

147

for myself, even if I wasn't in bother with her at all. Being a nice guy made me feel better, and that was all I wanted. I'd try to spend some quality time with them, going back to nature and all things beautiful. We got some happiness there; it wasn't all bad. Once I felt better about myself I'd be gone again, the demons forgotten.

During my peak, the wife didn't seem to mind my drinking. She wasn't suffering. I was making enough and she was short of nothing. I bought her drink as well. The kids were small and didn't know the difference. The mother-in-law bitched, but we just ignored her.

Business increased and the boss was happy. He just cared about the bottom line. Didn't we all. Most of the customers were sound, they were like myself, nice guys who liked a drink. These guys will always be nice guys. In many ways I don't regret any of these encounters. I got to know peple in a way that otherwise would have been impossible. I learned a lot about human nature and I learned a lot about myself. I made a lot of genuine friendships during those days, and these have remained. Of course, it wasn't really necessary for me to drink in order to make these friendships, all it would have taken was for me to drop my guard. At any rate, what's done is done and I don't regret making friends, regardless of what it took to make them.

It was as if I'd been drinking all my life. I just wanted to party. When the demons came I dealt with them; I didn't like them but I had no choice. They came as part of the package. I was well liked by the people who mattered, because they knew I was genuine and would harm nobody. I liked a drink but there was no malice. At company functions I was no longer an outsider; people were happy to spend their time with me. I had my fans for the first time in my life and it felt great. I knew they were only along for the ride and the minute the ride ended they would be gone, but I didn't care.

My pub career was going well and the mother-in-law was at bay. My queen behaved like the rest of them and used to ring the pub when my dinner was ready. I was normal like everyone else, with all the ducking and diving and everything that goes with it. It's sad to think that I counted the fact that the barman asked me if I was there when the phone rang as one of the highlights of my drinking career, signalling that I was normal. I was normal all right: a normal maniac.

Then the queen got pregnant again, and my peak started to end. The pressure of two kids, one still a baby, and another on the way was all a bit too much. I started spending even more time at the pub, not because I wanted to but because I needed to.

Lodgers

My aunt was married to a bastard. He hadn't drunk in years, but he was still a bastard. She had left him a few times, kids and all. This time she didn't just leave, she ran. My old lady took her in. It's funny really; she wouldn't have taken me in, she'd have left me on the street, but she could take in my aunt and all the cousins. She was stuck for two beds, so we took two of the cousins. We had two kids of our own and another one due, a huge mortgage, my drinking and we now had two teenagers as well. It was the worst thing we ever did, but then again it accelerated the process and that can't be bad. To go into hell and come out of it as quick is a lucky thing. The intensity might be greater, but a slow painful death would be worse.

The queen was thrilled, she had a live-in baby-sitter. She was no longer tied to the house like all the other women and she could party the nights away with me at the pub. My wife is a strong woman. She's not an alky, but she likes a drink and she's well able for it. She can drink as good as any man and maybe better. However, although she knows when to stop, when she was with me there was no reason to. I have never seen a woman drink like her and she is the envy of many a bored housewife. But it wasn't the drinking that was the problem, it was the getting out of bed the following day.

We started going to the pub together. We had gone there together before, but now she became a regular like me. No one seemed to mind. The other regulars only brought their queens every Sunday, but they were real queens in a wifey sort of way. My wife was one of the lads and she soon became an honorary Maurice. The publican loved her. He was used to looking at dirty dishevelled men stinking of BO, straight off a building site. The wife was a breath of fresh air for him. She was good looking and young, just the type of client he wanted. Also, her family had money, and even though she didn't have any herself she had the name of it, and the name was enough. Whilst she was going to his pub its value increased. He knew it and so did everyone else.

The publican was a funny fish. He had a peculiar manner and rarely smiled. He was shy really, and that's how it manifested itself. I liked him. He saw through the bullshit. He wielded power, though not deliberately. The customers pandered to him because they needed him, but he was above all that because he liked a drink himself. He was an ordinary man struggling to find his way, the same as the rest of us. He also had a conscience – the only publican I ever met with one. There were some who would take the money out of a sleeping man's pocket, but this fella wouldn't do such a thing. He often had a quiet word with me, telling me to watch myself. He couldn't do any more. He'd showed that he cared and that's enough for me. I just wish that I'd listened to him on some of those occasions. He used to warn me about the sharks. It was as if he knew that I just wanted to belong.

The publican warned me a few times about one fella and when I eventually listened it was nearly too late. I did listen though, so he hadn't been wasting his time completely. This Maurice was the biggest martyr for drink in the town, not to mind the pub. He could drink Guinness until the cows came home, and I only knew him to fall down once. When he fell he had no drink taken, he was just on his way for it. He got weak crossing the bridge after four weeks of solid drinking. He was a mouthy rogue who was always on the look-out for victims. He'd get the fools drunk and then make them pay. It was all about ego: he wanted to be big. He is really, so I won't dispute it. He's the king of Guinness drinkers, and a noble sovereign he is too in many ways. The strange thing about the wife was that she enjoyed playing with his majesty and his subjects. I couldn't understand it, because she's an intelligent woman who rules a far greater kingdom of her own.

One Sunday I went to the pub for a post-mass pint – even though I hadn't been to mass. Pud was with me as usual. It was only twelve-thirty, but the place was packed. I soon discovered that they were all going to Cork on a coach to watch a match. The king of Guinness asked me if I would like to go along and, after thinking about it for ten seconds or so, I decided I would. I rushed home with Pud and was back in the pub again in no time with a cheque for a hundred quid cashed in my pocket.

We left for Cork in the milling rain and made a few stops along the way for fear we might get dehydrated. When we arrived at Musgrave Park, the rugby ground, we met our team leaving in another coach, as the match had been called off due to the weather. The king was delighted and immediately recruited my good self to direct us to a suitable tavern in the vicinity. I was delighted as well not to have to sit through an entire match when all I wanted was a barrel of porter.

I took them off to Blarney and the Muskerry Arms, a fine tavern, known for its good drink. The king started supplying me with drink, a wink accompanying every pint. I did of course notice that none of the pints were full and therefore had been stolen off the settling tray. I didn't care much, so long as I wasn't caught. The money was staying in my pocket, thereby ensuring another day on the piss.

We got home just in time for last orders and the blow-in and my wife were there to greet us. I was completely wasted, and everyone thought it was great fun that the first match I had ever gone to was called off. The following day I went to cure myself and I met up with the king again. He told me it was my turn to buy because he had supplied the drink the day before. The hundred quid didn't last the day.

The Inner Sanctum

Because the publican valued the wife's custom, he allowed us to stay after hours. To stay back for a drink meant you had entered the inner sanctum – only the best were allowed in. The blow-in was asked in once, because of my queen, but he was refused at a later date and never readmitted. However, he still drank there during normal hours, something I'd never do if I'd been turned away.

The night the publican asked us back, I thought I had truly arrived. It was a great occasion. In my heart I knew it was because of the wife, but I didn't care, I was in, and that's what mattered. We stayed until the small hours and the window was tapped several times. Rat a tat tat, tat tat. A lesser mortal was dispatched to the side door to screen the new arrival. Another Maurice would appear and more drinks were started.

All night the crowd changed. Some were on their way home from work. Others were coming from discos. Some were still at work, just having a break. I thought it was all great fun and I got absolutely pissed, but the queen weathered it well. The publican got drunk, and she humoured him very successfully. She ruled the night and all men were put to shame. I was very proud of her. It was the first time ever that I had been sick in the toilets and yet resumed drinking as if nothing had happened.

The wife is a great driver as well. To be a great driver is one thing, but to be a great drunk driver is an even greater advantage. Out the road we went, pissed as coots, and turned left down to our house. We fell into bed and didn't wake until the afternoon. My cousin played mammy. The queen was quite sick. She was pregnant, after all.

When I woke I felt terrible and was very empty. The day was gone, and I was lonely for it. I never liked losing a day. Rats are nocturnal creatures, but I'm not a rat. Fear gripped me and suddenly the honeymoon was over – I looked at myself and hated what I saw. I didn't like hating myself. I looked at the kids and hated myself even more. I felt a strong sense of being in the wrong. My wife didn't look like a queen and I didn't want her to be one anymore. I just wanted her to be my wife. I wanted to be normal. But it was too difficult. I couldn't handle it. I got dressed and went to the pub. The abnormal was becoming normal.

Guinness is my drink, but on a raw empty stomach it can be too much. I'd seen the Maurices drink a can of cider to settle the system and I drank one then. Once the cider was finished I called a pint. No one said anything. The unspoken words, conveyed in a glance, were enough. Everyone was in pain, and together we cured it. We all drank silently and slowly until the glow returned. Then we began to talk and our pain was soon forgotten. My children were my source of pain, and I forgot them. Later on the queen appeared, no longer a wife, and the party started again. However, the buzz was gone for me and it never returned.

Demons

The baby was born and I was in a bad way. A severe urgency rose from deep inside me and I was drinking heavily whenever I could. When I couldn't I was depressed. I knew I desperately needed to take action, but I couldn't seem to do anything about it. I was helpless and just needed drink. I didn't know nor care what was happening to me. My cousin stayed at home with the kids and I went straight from work to the pub. Whenever she could, the wife joined me. My family had long since ceased to be an issue. I didn't give a shit about them, nor they me. I had my cousin and that was all I needed. I didn't really need her either, but she was handy for the wife and when the wife was happy I was left alone. The Maurices noticed the change in me. They looked at me and wondered. I was showing all the signs of going over the line.

Christmas came and went and I hardly noticed. I was on autopilot. The baby was christened and the publican warned me again. He told me I'd kill myself, but I didn't listen. I continued doing the only thing I knew how.

I needed the drink, but I didn't want it. I wanted to stay at home and be with the kids. Pud was mad about me and I about her. I was mad about the other two as well, but they were smaller. Whenever I woke up and didn't have to go to work, I'd get depressed. The kids would look at me and I'd hug them and hope to have the strength to stay with them, but the drink was ruling. I often left, almost biting the steering-wheel, the rage building, needing the drink but wanting the kids.

I knew what it was to be a child. I knew how it could hurt. It shouldn't hurt, but it often does. Fathers are supposed to make everything better, but I knew I was the cause of the hurt. That tore at me more than anything. The wide innocent eyes of a child crying out for love and not getting it. I swore I'd never do it to mine, but I was, and it was killing me.

When I'd been drinking, my ability to rationalise in favour of myself was astounding. After five or six pints nothing mattered anymore. The pain was gone – until the demons of slumber returned in an unforgiving onslaught. I tried in vain to recapture that time when the drink made everything seem better. I searched for that window in time when I could consume just the right amount of alcohol and the world and everything in it was wonderful. That was a great place to be and I longed for it, but the more I searched the further I drifted, until that for which I was searching became but a distant memory, and eventually I wondered had I ever found it at all. And so the cycle continued, never better only worse.

Prayer

Monday afternoon, and the glass in front of me is almost empty.

I pick it up.
I look at it.
I stare blankly at the trail of dried froth as it details every sip, every gulp. Like the rings on a tree, it tells its age. Without thought for its servant, it signals to all my state of mind.

The distance between rings at first is small; age discernible only by the darkness of the yellow rings. Once pure and white, the froth has aged with time, and as it travels lower, on the interior of my tulip-shaped glass, towards the remnants of its great glory, its virginal purity is once again visible, exalting its greatness while mocking its unworthy servant, unable to conclude its life with the dignity it demands.

The ability to consume its power has left me.

I crave desperately for its magical spirit to envelop me, to fan the dying embers of my soul, to instil in me its power, to release me from the bondage it has condemned me to.

I must be strong.

I know my black-and-white master will eventually show mercy

My master's voice tells me from somewhere deep within 'Don't despair, I will save you.'

How long more do I need to suffer?
Have I not repaid yesterday's kindness with hours of sleepless torment?
I have rejected the God of my youth.
I have abandoned my dreams, turned my back on my family, and all in favour of my master in the glass.

I have defended him against attack, the incessant and unforgiving onslaught from those who have yet to find peace within his magical spell.

I have sought converts to pay him homage, and yet he refuses to release me.

I am his greatest disciple and, unlike the disciples of that God of my youth, I have never denied him.

His voice tells me to take him, to pour his black redemption into my soul, and he will release me from within, he will free me of my torment and make me one with himself.
He tells me that a master as great as he will never forget a servant as noble as I.

I take him in my hands.
I bless him.
I revere him.
I pray to him for help.
He will not forsake me, for I am his and he is mine.
We are one, bound together for all eternity.
I praise you my black master and I love you. I shall never deny you.
I place my glass to my dry lips, and I drink.

I drink and I drink.

The rich and beautiful black-and-white master lubricates my hungry mouth.
He flows down over my tonsils and onwards towards the depth of my being.

The ritual complete, I place my empty glass on the counter in front of me.

My eyes are open and wild, and I feel naked, vulnerable, afraid.
My master is gone, the counter before me is naked and bare.

I feel the burning eyes of my fellows penetrating me.

I feel so alone, I need my master to return.

I look at the old woman on the other side of the bar, who is sitting unceremoniously in the tabernacle of my God, invested with unworthy authority to disperse his power to his willing servants.

I lift the decaying glass which once held the glory of my lord.

I pass it to the old woman. She removes it from my shaking hand and, with a shameful lack of reverence, places it in a decrepit tray, decrepit like her, only to be washed clean in the stainless steel frame in that unkempt corner of my god's humble home.

*   *   *

My hand steadies
A long drink, and my mind steadies
The dim light of control is once again visible
Another drink
The light fades

Guilt – it's overwhelming.
I think of the children. Their innocent vibrant faces
appear before me like the demons of drunken slumber
Their green, blue and brown eyes plead for my return,
arms outstretched they forgive unconditionally, while
their smiles challenge the need, the devil.

War is declared.

The devil below has travelled north, to the sanctity of my mind.
Need fights want; need is winning.

The old woman is gone, a young one stands in her place.
Expensive, healthy, together, she stands, administering
the blackness that is the devil, camouflaged in his veil of purity.

The devil stands before me.
Images – images of choice – flit before me.
The mirror, nestled on the wall of hell,
Reflecting the urgency.

The final choice.
Life or death.
The devil demands.
The children plead.

I fight him, but his conquest is complete.
Another drink.
The fight is lost.
The children fade, my life fades with them.

End of the Road

The madness of it! The middle of the afternoon and I'm in a prick of a pub. It's total lunacy. Just hold on a minute. What exactly am I doing wrong?

I'm starting to talk to myself again. I hope nobody is looking; I'd better make sure my lips aren't moving or everyone will know how bad I am. Go easy on yourself.

I don't care. Yes I do. This is wrong!

No it's not, it's quite fucking normal! Why shouldn't I be here? I'm not the only one. The wasters at the other end of the bar, they're the ones that shouldn't be here. They have no jobs, no wives, no one to look after. Why do they need to be here? I have a job. Christ, do I have a job! My wife is well taken care of. The kids have everything they need. I'm only having a few pints. Stop feeling guilty, you're entitled to a few drinks.

I look at my pint again. Where would I be without you, you beautiful mind saving porter? I pick up the nearly empty glass, give it a swish, point it to the woman behind the bar, and – ah! – down the hatch!

My eyes are locked on my empty glass. I tell myself that I can get up now, before it's too late, and walk out of here. Guilt! It's back again. If only I could think of something else, but I can't.

I start to reason with myself. I can get into my car and drive out towards home, to my wife and children. I've only had three pints. Sure, that's nothing. Maybe I'll just have one more. She has it pulled anyway. I'll have this and I'll go home then. I'll be home in plenty of time for dinner. I'll put the kids to bed and, afterwards, I might even take the queen for a drink. That's it. Stop breaking your own balls. Relax. Have a fag, for Christ's sake.

The barwoman is asking me for £1.90. I raise my head from my empty glass, a new, fresh pint of Guinness greets my vacant stare. Yeara, what the hell, I could be dead tomorrow. I lean back on my stool and reach into my pocket. I feel for some change, but there is nothing there. Where did that tenner go? Jasus, you'd want to be shiting money!

I search my jacket pocket for the wallet that the mother-in-law bought me last year when she was in Italy. A wallet my bollocks! No fear of her putting a £50 note into it. She'd prefer it if I dropped dead. Then her only daughter would be free of this evil bastard. She would love it. The two merry widows drinking Irish coffees.

I find my wallet in my inside pocket. I take it out, open it and remove a crisp £20 note. I give a quick glance to make sure there are another few in there. Three more. And why wouldn't there be? Wasn't I only at the bank two shagging hours ago ? Still, it's safer to check. You never know what could happen. It would be a terrible thing for a man to be in a public house and run out of money. I don't forget the last time it happened. I had to ask the old wagon behind the bar for twenty quid, then I had to hand it back to her when she gave me the pint. Jasus, that was the pits! I never felt so low. To make matters worse, the wrinkled old bitch told everyone that I was stuck for money, and of course she had to make out that things must be bad at home. I won't forget her for that, I'll get her yet!

No, it's safer to make sure that I have enough money on me.

I mean, a man like me could meet an important customer and I'd need to buy him a drink. I could fall into company and have to stand a round. What would people say if I couldn't pay my way?

I throw the £20 note onto the bar. Like a vulture starved of meat after weeks in a dry desert, the old bitch appears and swipes the money. I watch her as she hobbles her miserly way to the till. She slips my crisp hard-earned note into her rusty old till, begrudgingly removes my change and turns, slowly, in my direction. She places the change from my note on the counter and stares me in the eye, saying to herself – don't worry, sonny, I'll have the rest before long. I tell myself that she will in her dreams. As soon as I finish this pint I'm out of here.

I raise my black pint with its beautifully moulded white creamy top to my lips, my back straightens, my head tilts back and, as the pride of Dublin flows back lubricating my tonsils, my eyes close and for a moment in time I rejoice in the mercy of God. I open my eyes and I withdraw the glass from my lips. I place it on the counter in front of me to allow it a few moments of well-deserved rest. As I position my frame in a comfortable slouch against the bar, my gaze settles uneasily on the mirror behind the bar.

I shift in my seat and attempt to focus my eyes on something else. Anything will do. Postcards from travelling patrons, a map of the ancient city, even the old bitch herself. All my efforts fail. They have been failing for what seems like an eternity. I know it's useless to fight it – day-dreaming into a mirror is a normal part of life. It's all I have left. Sometimes it's even fun.

It wasn't always like this. There was a time –it seems so long ago – that I could raise my glass to my image and smile a broad smile. Why can't it be like that now? Where did I go wrong? If only I could have those days back, when the 'pride of Dublin' made everything seem all right. Those were the days when a shy young man could walk into a pub and, after a few pints of mind-saving porter, become vivacious, strong and master of all he surveyed.

Yes, those were the days – carefree days – when the only person to consider was myself. I could go where I liked, do what I liked, say what I liked. If anyone were to interfere, I just told them to fuck off. If that didn't work, I fucked off. I was in control, nobody else. It seems such a long time ago, at the back of my mind like some intangible memory, more like a dream.

I had energy then. I was always on the move, going somewhere, doing something, getting on with the struggle to survive. I needed nobody, except when they had something I wanted. When I got it, I'd be gone, back on my journey to independence, where nothing would hurt me and nobody could control me.

Reluctantly, I look deep into the accursed mirror. I stare at the man who is staring back at me. I hate his pitiful face, his sad brown eyes, his receding hair. I take a gulp of my pint, never losing contact with the mirror. I stare at myself with a numbness of mind and body. I take another gulp of porter. I want to scream at this pitiful bastard. I want to tell him how he has ruined my life, my dreams, my very soul.

I hear someone calling me. I think it's my father. Is it him, come to save me? Has he remembered me? I want it to be him, come to take me home and mind me, to protect me, and to pick me up and cradle me with his massive frame, as he used to do before he went away. Jesus, where is he? Why can't he come and take me away and show me what to do?

I hear my name again. Someone is telling me to snap out of it. Snap out of what? I'm looking at myself. My lips are moving. I am telling the mirror that I hate myself, that I despise every bone in my miserable obese body. I am wishing myself the most humiliating death imaginable. Someone is shaking me. I turn away from the mirror and look to my left and I see my friend's face. His eyes are wide with fear and he is pleading with me to talk to him. How can I talk to him? How can he understand what I am thinking? Nobody understands.

I am frightened now. I have reached the end and it's time to be honest with myself. I can no longer cheat my very soul. I decide I will end it all. I am thinking of nobody but myself. After all, nobody has thought of me.

My friend hands me a brandy. He tells me to drink it, that I will feel better. I drink it. My mind goes blank.

*   *   *

Morning. I was awake, but my eyes were still closed. I didn't know where I was, so I was afraid to open them. I tried to remember where I'd been, but I couldn't. I didn't know whether I'd driven the car or not. I didn't even know where the car was. I felt awful. My head hurt and my mouth was dry. I tried to move my tongue, but it was stuck to my gums. I tried to lubricate it, but I couldn't. I needed water; badly.

I wondered if I should open my eyes. I knew it was dark, but the curtains could be drawn. It might be daytime. Did the wife know where I was? Was she beside me? Oh, sweet Jesus! That's it! I'm never drinking again.

I opened my left eye, the one closest to the pillow. That was the safest one in case anyone was looking. The room was dull, but it wasn't dark. I knew then that it was daytime. That meant trouble. The queen had a head start. I opened my right eye and I saw the mirror. The stupid god-forsaken bastard that built the house had put mirror doors on the wardrobe. There was nothing worse than looking at yourself first thing in the morning – or afternoon, or whatever the hell it was.

I tried to move and my head hurt me. I could see my jeans and wondered if there was any money left. I shifted one leg out of the bed, then the other, and sat up. I was shaking. Then I started sweating.

The queen wasn't around. I grabbed my jeans and found some money. Then I found the keys of the car. Where in hell was the car? I looked in the mirror and felt pity for what I saw. I couldn't look any more. I needed water. I walked to the bedroom door, went out and turned right into the bathroom. I turned on the tap and wet my lips. I felt a bit better and walked to the boxroom and looked out the window. The car was there. The side I could see wasn't damaged. I prayed the other side wasn't either.

I went back to the bathroom and tried to be sick. It hurt, and nothing came. I turned on the shower and got under it. I was cold, but I was sweating. The shower made me feel better, but I was still afraid. I thought I heard a noise and I tried to get sick again, but nothing came.

I dried off and found clean clothes – I fell in love with the wife for a moment. Then I wondered where she was. I wondered should I get help and decided I should. I got dressed and went downstairs. The wife and the cousin were sitting there smoking and drinking coffee. Nobody spoke. I looked at the clock; it was one-thirty. I knew where I could get help, so I said goodbye. Nobody answered.

I checked the other side of the car; it was fine. I let out a long sigh. I was lonely now. The pressure wasn't as bad. I drove away to get some help. On the way I passed the pub and I was feeling bad so I decided to go in, to settle myself.

'A can of cider, please,' said I.

'You'll kill yourself,' he said, and he gave me the can.

I drank it slowly and in silence. There were others there, but nobody spoke. The publican was sick too, so he said nothing either.

*   *   *

The summer came and went, but I never even saw it. I knew that things had to change. If I could have stayed off the drink for a couple of days, things would have improved. The nights were long and that was unbearable. I had to do something with the nights. I had to stay busy until the pubs closed. I was drinking every day. If I could leave it to every two or three days it would be great. I was pissed every night. People were talking.

I decided I'd drive a taxi. I told everyone I needed the money. In a way it was true, but if I stopped drinking I wouldn't need extra money. I decided I'd do up the house with the extra money. That way the plan would work and I wouldn't drink the money. I told the wife and she seemed happy. She was on a downer too, but that was because of me. If I improved so would she.

The fella I drove the taxi for was a total waster. He worked days and I did the nights. All he wanted from me was money. He never spent any of it on the car – that was a heap of shit. The only reason I got the job was because nobody else would touch him.

The first week went great. I made a load of money. When the wife saw it she was delighted: a fine wad of notes. The second week was as good, I even made more. I met a Maurice on the Sunday night; he was a taxi driver as well. It was four in the morning and he said he was going for a pint. I decided I'd go with him. We went to the pub. Rat a tat tat, tat tat, and in we went. There were guards there, in uniform, and the craic was great. We drank our fill, and rightly so – we were hard-working men.

The following day was Monday. It was a bank holiday and I went on the piss. I got buckled, but I'd been off of the drink for four days. That was a long time. I went on the piss on Tuesday again, because all the Maurices that drove taxis did. I went again on Wednesday – because I had to. On Thursday I went back to work and that night I drove the cab. At three in the morning I went for a pint, guards and all. The plan was working well.

Christmas was coming and I had to work hard in the job. I had to work hard at the taxi driving as well. I also had to drink. However, my health wasn't able for it and I started to get sick.

Guinness is a rich drink. It's not coarse like lager. Lager cuts the stomach out of you. But Guinness burns the arse off you. My arse was on fire. I started to get piles. I didn't want to believe they were piles, but I was bleeding when I did a shit. There was more blood than shit and I thought I was going to die. I told everyone I had cancer.

I knew then I was in serious trouble. I started day-dreaming about my own death and my funeral. I could see everyone sympathising with the wife and saying what a nice fellow I was. I was clutching at anything to make me feel better. The only cancer I had was of the mind.

I went to the doctor and he gave me an injection. It helped for a while and I was able to sit again. My arse was very important in my work. I drove all day and I drove all night. If my arse wasn't right, I wasn't right.

Then, near Christmas, my eyes started giving me trouble. First I got a dendritic ulcer in the left eye and then one in the right one; then I got them in both. I had had them before, many years ago. It only happens when the immune system is shattered, and mine was in bits. I was going around like a blind man, wearing dark glasses and feeling my way. The sunlight was killing, so I only went out at night. That was all right for the taxi driving, but very difficult for the day job. However, I'm a tough bastard and I did them both. Fair play to me. The truth was, of course, that I didn't really know what I was doing.

I knew that my bad health was caused by the drink. I didn't admit it, however, even to myself. It took me a year off the drink before I could do that. The wife was demented, the cousin tormented, the kids didn't know what day of the week it was and the mother-in-law was doing novenas. I was just sick.

Christmas came and the money was good. I worked hard to wreck it for everyone. After Christmas everyone got sick. I was the worst. We all got chickenpox and they went into my eyes to keep the ulcers company. It was misery personified. Happy New Year, my bollocks!

I gave notice to the man with the taxi. I didn't like him anyway, nor anyone belonging to him. Anyway, I was a total mess. I went sick from my day job and went drinking instead. I was pissed for the month of January. The blow-in Maurice had to cut loose from me. A few of the other Maurices tried to talk to me, but I wasn't listening. The publican tried as well, but he was talking to the wall.

The queen was pissed off. She eased off on the drink and left me to get on with it alone. The mother-in-law started hanging around and the cousin was looking at me strangely. I was a truly miserable sight and I was breaking all my principles. I was a behaving like a proper bollocks, but I couldn't seem to help it. I tried to stop, but I couldn't. My standards had dropped so much that I didn't care what people thought of me anymore. I even started to envy people that were dossers, the useless gobshites that never did anything for anyone and thought of nobody but themselves. I wanted to give up the job and become a dosser.

The hangovers got worse. My arse was in an awful state and I could hardly see. Death felt imminent – or so it seemed. Everyone ran away from me. I prayed to the devil, but even he seemed to be gone. Nobody would help and, sure, who could blame them?

Conspiracy

January ended and February began. I tried to pull myself together. I went back to work and tried to drink less. I was in a financial mess and one of the Maurices said he'd help. In fairness to him he did. He spoke to the bank and we rearranged a few things. The pressure was off on that front, for another while at least.

I went to Dublin one Friday, around the 7th of February. I went on the train, because my eyes were bad. I'd been good for a week or so and the wife was talking to me again. The day went well and everyone at work was happy. When everyone was happy, so was I. I always liked to please people.

On the way home, I had a few drinks on the train. I rang the wife and arranged to meet and go for a drink. When I got back I went straight to a pub. I was feeling good and decided I deserved a few drinks on my own to relax. I had a few and I did relax.

The wife came to meet me and she was in foul humour. The cousin was with her. I don't know who was baby-sitting and I didn't care either. The wife started bitching and I bitched back. We went at each other hammer and tongs, and the cousin just stood and watched. The wife was behaving as if she was a distressed damsel, and I began to smell a rat. I was being set up. It was all too sudden.

Eventually she left and I started knocking the drinks back. I couldn't get them in fast enough. I realised now that it was the queen that was my problem. First it had been my family and now it was her. I'd soon fix the lot of them.

I got pissed and went for a curry. The Irish drunk would be lost without the chicken curry. I got my curry and went home. By then I was well pissed. The wife was still up and ready for a fight. Her mother had got to her. I tried to eat my curry, but her temper was running high. Then she threatened to have me thrown out of the house. She knew that would work and it did. No one was going to throw me out of my own house. I'd been thrown out of enough, but they weren't doing it to me where I was paying the bills.

I threw the curry across the floor and the wife rang her mother. I went mad. I pulled the phone off the wall, the wife hit the deck and I was roaring. Then I noticed Pud watching everything that was happening and her frightened little eyes were pleading with me to stop. I did; I had no choice. Pud had the power.

I went upstairs and got ready for bed. I knew I was nearly sober now, because I had started to hate myself. I heard the door open and footsteps in the hall. I went downstairs and there was a guard in the sitting-room. I tried to be a hard man, but I was pathetic really. The guard told me to go to bed and no messing or he'd take me to the station, and I did. The end was nigh.

I went on the piss on Saturday and on Sunday as well. I saw Pud on Monday and the love was gone. She didn't like me any-more. She said nothing, but I knew. She wasn't looking at her dad but at a beast she wasn't afraid of but didn't love either. She gave me back the power, and I wondered why. I left and went to work.

No one was speaking to me at home. The silence was evil. I went to work and then straight to the pub. I knew it wasn't right, but I went anyway. A Maurice named Martin came in with a camera, an unusual one that connected to a printer. He took my picture and went away and an hour later he came back and handed me my photo. I was shocked at my appearance. I drank another pint and continued to get drunk. But everything felt different. I sensed an air of finality.

I was home by nine. The wife was gone and the cousin was there. I was very drunk. The Maurice that was sorting things out for me at the bank called round and told me to sign something. I signed it and went to bed.

Court

Next morning the phone woke me. The wife answered it and got dressed in a hurry. She left and the cousin looked at me and shook her head. Something was up, I knew it.

I was sick again. My stomach was bad and my arse hurt. My head was numb from the drink and I couldn't think straight. I decided to go to work, and to try and sort myself out. I called on some of my old friends that day. They weren't able to help me, so I went away again. I decided to go home and not go to the pub. I went to the fish shop and bought some fish. It would do me good.

The mobile phone rang and it was the wife. She asked me to come home; she wanted to talk to me. I was going anyway, so it didn't matter. I wondered what she wanted to talk about, but she sounded pleasant, so I decided not to worry.

There was a squad car at the shop on the way to my house. There was only one guard in it and he looked at me. I didn't like his look and his eyes followed me. My stomach did a somersault and I was afraid. I got to my house and my wife's car was there. I parked and went in. I stood in the hall and there was silence. I started to shake. It felt empty, no children, and it was cold.

I opened the door into the kitchen. A guard stood there and I was trembling.

'You're Peter O'Flynn?' he asked.

'I am,' I replied.

'I have a notice here which I am now going to serve on you. Under the Domestic Violence Act, 1973, you are hereby prohibited from entering these premises or coming near your wife and children, without leave from the court. In short, Peter, you have five minutes to pack your clothes and other necessities and leave the house.'

He handed me a piece of paper with official writing on it. I was shaking like a leaf. I felt my mouth going dry. I touched my forehead to see if I was really awake. My stomach started jumping and wouldn't stop. Then I saw my wife. She looked beautiful, dressed in black as if in mourning. Her blonde hair was fixed to perfection, her make-up impeccable. I looked at her, my eyes pleading, but she just turned to ice and that frightened me.

'You've done it to yourself, Peter,' she said. Nothing more was needed.

The guard looked at me, and I think he felt sorry for me. He told me to sit down, but I couldn't.

'Can I get a drink of water?' I asked, standing in my own kitchen.

'I'll get it for you,' he said, his humanity showing. I drank it slowly and went upstairs, packed my bags and left.

I drove away, not knowing where to go. I was alone again and nobody wanted me. The crazy thing was that I had wanted to stop drinking for months. I had told my wife that I was going back to my old friends, but she wouldn't hear of it. I had wanted her to help me, but instead she had rejected me. I knew my behaviour was wrong, but I wasn't bad. I just needed love and support, some one to care for me, to help me. She knew about my past and my nightmares – the real ones. She knew of my fear of the street and returning to that degradation. She knew I had just wanted to belong. Knowing all this, she threw me out. It was more than I could take. It was the ultimate betrayal.

I called on my friend Seán. He was my oldest friend and was always there in a crisis. He rang my wife, but she wouldn't listen. I walked the floor, going mad. The tunnel was dark and there was no light at its end. I tried to get some sleep, but it wouldn't come. I couldn't face being homeless again. I'd been through enough and I wasn't going through any more.

When morning came I went to a hardware shop and bought a hose, some bonding tape and a knife. I drove for hours and went up into the mountains.

There is a remote plateau on a mountain that looks out over the valley where I come from. It's remote and beautiful in a desolate kind of way. I went there and looked across at my homeland. The river meandered beneath me and flowed towards the horizon to meet the sea. I longed to be part of it.

I connected the hose to the exhaust and, cutting it to the required length, brought it into the car. The key was in the ignition and I looked at it for what seemed like an eternity. I couldn't go on, I told myself. The battle was too great. I thought of the children, and myself as a child. I saw my helpless eyes looking at me in the window of time as I looked at my father. I wanted my father, but I was a man now, and he wouldn't come anyway. I thought of my children yet again.

I remembered the night years earlier when I had sat alone as everyone searched for my father. He lay dying on a nearby hillside, every tablet in the house consumed. I remembered the loneliness and the stillness and the cold. I could see my mother hugging my brother in the next room. I longed for a hug and I was cold. I asked for news of my father and I felt the blow to my face and the thumps to my back and I heard the screams of hatred ringing in my ears. I remembered crying myself to sleep and now I was crying again.

My father didn't die, but when he eventually came home he was taken away again, while I looked on, alone, my body trembling. I had always fought to survive, but now all my fight was gone. All the beatings returned to my memory. I felt my brother squeezing my testicles while I begged him to stop. I felt my mother pulling my hair and thumping my back. I saw my pants at my knees and felt the sweeping brush crack on my bones. I saw the fright in my own eyes, my mouth open screaming for mercy.

I crossed the pain threshold and went numb. I had had enough and I could take no more. It had to end, I had to make it end. I prayed to God for help and roared at him in anger. I wanted it to end, I couldn't fight anymore.

In my mind's eye I saw Pud's beautiful smiling face and her lust for life, and I cried. I saw Brownie, simple and beautiful, her brown eyes asking for love. I saw myself in her and I cried the more. Then I saw 'the terror', cuddly and strong, full of love, and I longed for a hug. I saw my home and saw that it was where I belonged, where I had belonged all along. My children stood before me and my childhood self stood with them. I was both myself and my father. My own brown eyes looked from the past and begged me to come home. I needed to be saved. As the ghost of my past faded in the light, I felt a power from deep inside myself.

Pud had given me the power. Now I knew why. I jumped from the car and shouted across the valley. I told them I loved them and that I was going to fight for them and for myself. I told them we were worth it, that the past was dead and buried. We had driven the demons out and together we would never let them return.

I took off the hose, started the car and drove towards home. The fight was on – the virus the enemy.